# VIETNAM – ONE S

*25th Infantry Division*

*Cu Chi Vietnam 1966-1967*

*Fredric A. Voto*

ISBN:1494332930
ISBN-13:9781494332938

DEDICATION

In Memoriam

Dedicated to my beloved family;
my mother Josephine, my father Alfred and my
most precious sister, Bonita (Bonnie)

Introduction

*"Vietnam ... One Soldier's Experience" reveals my deep personal struggles with fear, patriotism, authority, fidelity, racism, life, death, conscience, faith, justice, human tragedy and suffering.*

*Although Vietnam may be the forgotten war, it remains relevant because America is just emerging from two wars, Iraq and Afghanistan. On the horizon are Syria and Iran.*

*- from the Author*

## COMMENTS FROM READERS

*"It is a story that comes from the heart rather than an historical or chronological detail of war events."*

*One reader recognized that "the author always saw through events and saw the person."*

*Another reader saw it as "a gift ... 'I opened it and immediately started to read. I could not put it down. It was so very well written that I felt I was sharing the experiences with you."*

*"... I read every word and through your writing felt the horror of war and aftermath for those who served our country and sacrificed so much."*

*"This is an excellent read that takes you through the experience that was so real that I felt I was there with Fred.*

*It was an emotional roller coaster ride for me and made me appreciate this terrible experience called, The Vietnam Conflict.*

*One reader summed it up as "powerful and poignant..."*

## ACKNOWLEDGMENTS

First and foremost I wish to thank God for his protection and deliverance. I would like to thank my wife Helene for her encouragement and support during the writing of my Vietnam memoir.

I would also like to thank my step-son Paul Henry Desjarlais for "telephoning" me every Veteran's Day to thank me for my military service. Through Paul's personal interest I now have a sense of pride instead of shame for my service in Vietnam.

I thank my next door neighbor Jan Warren for her technical and creative editing skills.

I especially wish to thank Sgt. Belcher and Sgt. Terrian both of whom I managed to contact through the internet. Sgt. Terrian kindly gave me permission to use his photographs; some of which are included in this work. Each has contributed to the accuracy of certain recollected details.

Lastly I acknowledge and thank all those with whom I was privileged to serve. I remain forever and deeply humbled towards those who gave so much more.

## The Long Journey

The early evening flight from Boston to Oakland, California was long. When we landed the night was pitch black. We arrived sometime around midnight.

I had always wanted to take a trip to California but I had in mind somewhere a bit more romantic than Oakland. Perhaps someplace like San Francisco, Los Angeles or San Diego. There was nothing to see at the moment on this darkest of nights. The airport was nearly empty of travelers. All the shops were closed. I walked alone to a deserted part of the terminal to await my connecting flight.

## A Look Back

I had met Janice when I was 17 years old. It was love at first sight. I knew right then and there I wanted her to be my wife. That was before she entered Catherine Laboure School of Nursing and I entered Boston College. How fast those four years of college had gone by.

The military draft was still in force in the mid sixties. I joined the R.O.T.C. (Reserve Officer Training Corp) because enlisted men could not bring their spouses with them on active duty, at least not initially.

As a reserve officer I had to serve two years of active duty and then six years of reserves. By becoming a 2nd Lieutenant, I could take my wife with me. This strategy worked perfectly into our plans to be married immediately after graduation. R.O.T.C. was a new experience; wearing a military uniform, being part of a precision drill team, and best of all, after summer camp at Fort Devens in my senior year I was a Distinguished Military Student and had achieved the high rank of cadet Lieutenant Colonel. During the three-week summer camp between junior and senior year we fired live rounds with the M1 rifle. We lived in old army barracks and had strict inspections every day. When camp was over, Janice and her Dad came to pick me up. I felt very proud that I had successfully completed summer camp. All we needed to do now was to get through senior year.

*Senior prom … 1965*

*Reserve Officer Training Corps Uniform - April, 1962*

I would earn my commission in the Infantry as a 2nd Lieutenant.
I originally selected Infantry as my military occupational specialty
(MOS) then changed to the Finance corps.  I changed back again
to Infantry for two reasons – one noble and one out of pure ego.
I thought if a man were to be fighting for his country then he ought

to be in the fight – that was the noble reason. Secondly, I did not like the Finance insignia and was impressed with the crossed rifles on my uniform lapel. I changed my MOS back to Infantry. That was my ego. Senior year brought with it many proud moments with the R.O.T.C. As seniors we were entitled to buy our own tailor made uniforms. We bought them from Allied Uniforms in Boston. We bought dressed blues as well. The uniforms looked so sharp. We wore them to the Senior Military Ball.

Commencement Day finally arrived and I received my Army commission as a second lieutenant along with my Bachelor's Degree. Janice and I were married right after graduation, June 19, 1965.

I already had orders to attend the Infantry Officer's Basic Course. I reported for active duty at Fort Benning in Columbus, Georgia July 19, 1965. We managed to rent a small four - room apartment just off post, number 6 Wilson Drive. It was our first apartment together. At last we were on our own.

Because Jan was a registered nurse she was able to get a job at St. Francis Hospital in Columbus. We planned to save the money she earned and try to live on my salary of $600 a month.

*Our Wedding Day – June 19, 1965*

**Infantry Officer's Basic Course (I.O.B.C.)**

The Infantry Officer's Basic Course consisted of eight weeks of classroom training as well as field training. We attended classes in tactics and map reading etc. We drove tanks, armored personnel carriers and jeeps. We fired various small arms weapons with live ammunition and crawled under barbed wire while being machine gunned over our heads with live ammunition. That was to teach us to keep our butts down.

We had lots of PT (Physical Training) but the most challenging of all events was POW (Prisoner of War) camp. The objective was to be dropped off by trucks into the woods and to find our way back to a rallying point along a road without being captured. They trucked us out at night. Some of us thought we'd escape capture if we jumped over the side of the truck before they reached their drop-off point. As the truck slowed down several of us jumped over the side and ran into the woods.

Our small group was soon separated and scattered into the dark night and even darker woods. I quickly found myself alone. I became disoriented. Suddenly I heard the sound of dogs barking. They were using attack dogs to hunt us down! The closer they came, the faster I ran until I tripped, stumbled, and rolled down into a gully. I rolled into some brambles and underbrush. By the time I extricated myself from the thorny underbrush the dog's fierce teeth were about two inches from my nose. His snarling face was so ferocious! I just hoped the handler was not going to let him go. They tied my hands behind my back and took me off to the POW camp. I spent the whole night being interrogated and harassed. We were caged in pens. I learned that if you kept your mouth shut they didn't pay as much attention to you. One officer acted tough and he found himself with his legs wrapped tightly around a pole. A soldier then stood on his thighs. That officer actually ended up seriously injured. Finally at 3 or 4 a.m. they released us. We ran westerly through underbrush and swamp until we reached the rally point. All I could think of was, "Oh my God, what if this were for real?"

## Airborne School

I signed up to go to airborne school right after I graduated from I.O.B.C. Airborne school was more physically demanding but much more fun. The program consisted of three phases: ground week, tower week and jump week. We did Parachute Landing Falls "PLF'S" until we could fall in any direction whichever direction the parachute would be traveling; backward, forward or sideways. Jumping from the towers was great fun; first the thirty-four foot tower, then the two-hundred foot tower. It reminded me of Coney Island in New York. *"Stand up, hook up, shuffle to the door, jump right out and count to four!"* This became our mantra. We sang it on our daily runs. We practiced "PLF'S" over and over and over again.

There were plenty of pushups for those who couldn't get it right. My first jump was a bit scary because I didn't know what to expect. We lined up within the aircraft, one row of men or "stick", as they were called, was on each side. Once the light came on, the sergeant at the door hurried us forward, one by one, as we swiftly shuffled out the door.

When my turn came to jump I pushed my static line forward to the sergeant who gathered it in with all the others. I took my jump position at the door. I jumped high, up and out. Then I counted one 1000, two 1000, three 1000, four 1000. By that time my parachute opened and I was free of the aircraft. The wind from the propellers of the C-130 forced my body parallel to the ground then I straightened vertically, my feet toward the ground.

My risers were twisted round each other. I pulled them in opposite directions separating them just like I was taught. I spotted the LZ (Landing Zone) and pulled my risers so the wind would push me closer to the rally point. It's a long walk carrying a heavy silk T10 parachute, harness and all. The drift down was an exhilarating experience. The treetops were getting closer. It was time to prepare myself for my PLF. I hit the ground a little harder than I expected but I made a perfect PLF. I was on my feet in seconds. The next four jumps went pretty much the same only I hit the ground differently each time because of the direction and velocity of the winds. My classmate and neighbor broke his leg. Otherwise, we all made it through and were awarded our jump wings. I had qualified as a parachutist.

## Headquarters Detachment

After jump school I was assigned to a Headquarters Detachment at Fort Benning, Georgia as an S4 Supply Officer. What did an infantryman know about supplies? Absolutely nothing! I was placed in charge of supply as well as the mess hall. The respective NCO's (non-commissioned officers) of each area took care of the day-to-day business. I implemented the wishes of the commanding officer and tried to settle trivial complaints and issues. It was boring in every sense. The only highlight was winning a special certificate for the annual Savings Bonds Program.

## Jan Becomes Ill

One day my wife, Jan, became ill with vomiting. I drove her to St. Francis Hospital. We thought perhaps she had the flu. I sat in the waiting room as the doctor and the nurses took her in for assessment and to run tests. Some time had passed when the doctor finally came out. He said, "I'm sorry to tell you this but your wife is pregnant." "Sorry, I said, I'm delighted - that's wonderful." Many couples were using birth control at that time but we were strict Catholics. We returned to our apartment. I felt a very special warmth and tenderness toward Jan. We called our families back home in Massachusetts to share the good news. As a result of Jan's constant morning sickness she was unable to continue working. The money we had hoped to save was never realized.

Days turned into weeks and the weeks into months and then one evening Jan went into labor. It was urgent now. She could hardly walk to the car. I tried to remain calm. Our daughter Michelle was born on April 6, 1966. She was the most beautiful baby. I was overwhelmed because it was like seeing my own reflection in a mirror. Just on the other side of the glass of the nursery a little pink card read, "Voto …girl". I was never so proud or so happy. After a brief stay at the hospital, Jan was released to go home.

We had left our tiny apartment on Wilson Drive as a couple. We returned home as a family. Michelle delightfully consumed our lives which had changed so much in such a short time. How thrilling it was to be a father. Janice's mom and aunt came down from Massachusetts to Georgia by train to visit us and to hold the first grandchild of the family. We named her Michelle Marie – born April 6. 1966.

*Michelle Marie at 4 months old…*

I was proud of what we had accomplished together, especially since we came from rather poor backgrounds. My parents had not even finished high school. They were children of Italian immigrants. I looked forward to completing my active duty and moving on to civilian life. Hopefully we would be blessed with more children. Janice was a registered nurse and I had a college degree. The prospects for our future looked bright.

My orders were to go to Korea for my second year of active duty. After that I would be out with six years of reserves to complete my military obligation. It sounded exotic to go to Korea. I had never been out of the country. I knew of other lieutenants who had gone to Korea or Germany and they described wonderful experiences. I was looking forward to seeing more of the world, which up until now was somewhat parochial. My life experience was limited and not very adventuresome. I had lived with my mother, father and sister, Bonnie, in a small neighborhood in Roxbury just outside of Boston. Korea would be a real adventure.

### Long Journey Continues

As the plane landed in Oakland, memories of the last four years flashed through my mind. Memories of Jan's bridal shower, our wedding day, college, proms and military balls and all the happy times we spent with friends. I could not hold onto a single thought long enough to make it real again. I could see Michelle sleeping in the tiny crib at my mother-in-law's house in Dorchester.

The image of our baby left a fixed and indelible impression on my mind. She lay on her tummy. I gently patted her back while she slept so peacefully. I didn't know how to say good bye to my four-month old baby. How I wished I could still feel Jan's arms around me as we kissed, perhaps for the very last time

The Oakland airport terminal was deserted now. I checked the departures board for my connecting flight. I was waiting for the next flight to Hawaii, then to the Philippines. I was going to Vietnam. I was not deployed with a combat unit. I traveled alone, like any other traveler. Several friends who graduated before me had already been killed in this war. What would my chances be? Would I ever make it home again?

 My heart sunk heavily within me. Dazed and in disbelief, I now felt the painful grip of emptiness. I sat on the floor; leaned my back against the wall and fell asleep. My flight was scheduled to depart the next morning.

Daybreak came and with it the terminal awakened to its usual hustle and bustle. Passengers were running here and there, to this gate and to that gate. I confirmed my gate number and headed to my Continental airlines flight. I reached the gate in plenty of time. I boarded the aircraft and we were soon airborne. I had begun the second leg of my long journey. The plane landed in Hawaii. There was a short stay there so they let passengers disembark. I walked up to the store. I smoked Camel cigarettes so I lit up and bought a few more packs. I didn't know when I might get my next opportunity to buy cigarettes. Smoking was the only comfort for me now. Hawaii was beautiful what very little I could see of it surrounding the airport. The air smelled sweet and warm and inviting. Someday I wanted to return. Daydreaming, I boarded the airplane. The flight to the Philippines gave me more time to think, more time to sit in disbelief.

My mind wandered back to my old neighborhood in Roxbury. I recalled Louis and Johnny Sturniollo's grocery store at the corner of my street. I remember how proud I was walking passed their store wearing my military uniform on R.O.T.C. day. I thought of Nannina, the Italian lady across the street. She made homemade macaroni. I could almost smell the tomatoes and basil she grew in her garden. She was like a grandmother to me. I thought of my childhood friends. We played marbles, baseball and tag football together. I thought of the priests and nuns and the comforting smell of incense when I was an altar boy. Aside from my immediate family, would anyone be thinking of me? I seemed suspended in time. After the final leg of my journey we were over the skies of Vietnam. As we got closer, I could see the heavens light up like fireworks on the fourth of July. Flares illuminated the night sky.

Fiery explosions on the ground flashed bright in the darkness then quickly faded away. I was still safe at 30,000 feet but I knew that just below this airplane was death and destruction. The plane began its slow but steady decent. "Could we be shot out of the very sky?" We touched down at Tan Son Nuht Airbase in Saigon around 11:00 p.m. or midnight. I was tired from the long flight, a journey that lasted nearly 24 hours.

**Camp Alpha**

I was now joined by hundreds of other men at a place called Camp Alpha. We were herded like cattle to be made disposition of like so many sheep on market day. We were welcomed to Camp Alpha by an NCO. After some formalities he told us a little about the camp, what would transpire and how we would be assigned to units in the field. We were given a place to sleep for the night.

I was brought to a trailer or vehicle of some sort and given a blanket. There in the dark, alone, I spent my first night in Vietnam. I was scared and deeply longing for home.

How could I be so far away from the ones I loved so much? Would I ever see Jan or Michelle again? My mind was tormented by these thoughts. I wanted to cry out but no one could save me from this fate. Nature was merciful and covered me with a blanket of sleep until morning. I held my rosary tightly in my hand for comfort. My long journey had come to an end.

### Convoy to Cu Chi - 1966

I spent a couple of days at Camp Alpha. Finally I was given orders to join the 25th Infantry Division at Cu Chi, a town just northwest of Saigon. The convoy was to leave that day.

But how would I defend myself? I had no weapon. I felt very vulnerable. Highway 1 was relatively secure, or so I was told. In a very short time I had become distrustful and anxious. This distrust manifested itself in an embarrassing yet poignant way. Halfway along the journey the convoy stopped. I wanted to keep moving.

I didn't want to be a standing target. As soon as we stopped, children and women ran toward the convoy carrying all sorts of food and drink. Some food was in baskets, others, like soda, were in wooden cases. A little child ran quickly but directly towards me. I had heard stories of children being used by the Viet Cong to throw grenades or bombs at American soldiers. I ran to the opposite side of the truck and leaped over the other side onto the ground. I realized by the reaction of the driver and others who had made this trip back and forth to Saigon frequently that I had panicked and over reacted. I consoled myself with the fact that at least I was quick to recognize a possible threat. "How would I perform in combat if I am afraid of a mere child? ", I asked myself. The truth be told, I felt really stupid.

*Convoy to Cu Chi Base Camp...*

## The 25th Infantry Division

The 25th Infantry Division (*Tropic Lightning*) was based in Schofield barracks in Hawaii. They came over by ship as a unit. They arrived towards the end of April 1966, four months before I arrived. The 25th's area of responsibility was Cu Chi. The 2nd Battalion to which I was assigned was called, "*The Golden Dragons*". I came in cold. The men had experience together as a unit in Hawaii prior to arriving in Vietnam. Experience I sorely lacked. They also had shared initial combat experience that helped them bond.

My fellow officers had already distinguished themselves as veterans. The turnover rate among platoon leaders was very high. Many were killed or wounded. It was not unusual after six months of serving "on the line" that a new lieutenant replaced an outgoing officer. I was the new kid on the block. I was a 2nd Lieutenant or "butter bar" which referred to the gold colored pip worn on my shoulders. I felt very much an outsider. I knew I would have to prove myself in combat to gain their respect and to be accepted.

When the 25th Infantry initially entered Cu Chi I was told that they took heavy casualties of almost 50%. The Viet Cong were waiting for them. Cu Chi is well known for its myriad of VC tunnels, bamboo pits (pungi pits) and booby traps. The bamboo was sharpened at one end; the other end was fixed in the ground. It was then superbly camouflaged and the unsuspecting soldier would fall into the pit. The many sharp bamboo shafts would run through his body like spears.

The tunnels were so sophisticated they were actually used as hospitals where the VC brought their wounded. They were so well camouflaged they were invisible. I witnessed this first hand.

Some officers were relieved of duty because they froze in the heat of combat according to accounts related to me. Dazed and shocked, they were often trapped or ambushed. They saw their friends killed or wounded. Fear can take hold of a man and cripple his judgment or paralyze his mind.

These first-hand stories gave credence to the ferocity and bloodshed of the encounters.

Both sides suffered heavy losses. A particular scourge, I was told, was the notorious Hobo Woods, a Viet Cong stronghold. It was located not very far from our base camp.

## Arrival at 25th Division Headquarters

Upon arrival at the 25th Infantry Division Headquarters I was interviewed by some Major. He asked me about my military experience. I had no real experience as a rifle platoon leader.

I had only been a supply officer for one year. I hinted, when he asked my preference, that supply might be good for me based on my most recent assignment at Fort Benning. He was quick to remind me in a rather curt manner that what they needed were rifle platoon leaders. I already knew that so many of them were killed in action or wounded. He stared at the crossed rifles on my lapel. That was all he had to see. The interview ended abruptly. The major ordered transport for me to brigade headquarters.

That evening two officers took me in a jeep. They drove the jeep like it was a dune buggy speeding around the dirt roads. I didn't have any idea where I was or where we were going.

The nightmare just continued. We arrived at a tent that was set up as an officers' club. We ordered drinks. They and a couple of other officers who were there when we arrived seemed quite adapted to it all. There was the usual bar talk and jokes but I felt no levity whatsoever.

I liked a drink or two from my college days but I felt nauseous and in no mood for alcohol. Anxiety had set in my whole being in a big way. I didn't know anybody and I had no idea where we were.

I was never a macho man so I'm sure my conversation was a bit dull. I did all I could to hide my anxiety. The suspense, the change, and the unknown were quickly taking a toll on my emotions. All I could think about was that I had a whole year to try to stay alive. I eventually made my way to battalion headquarters and then to Company A. I was replacing a lieutenant who was in charge of the 2nd platoon. My company commander's name was Captain Clay. He was a West Point graduate, ranger-airborne type. Lieutenant Ogden was his executive officer. He was also a graduate of West Point. My impression was that some West Pointers did not hold R.O.T.C. graduates in very high esteem. I only hoped I could measure up to their expectations. Shortly after my arrival, Captain Clay was re-assigned and Lieutenant Ogden was promoted to Captain. He became our new company commander. These were the men under whom I served. Despite our differences in military education, I had a great deal of respect for both of them. They were competent leaders and that was all that really mattered.

### *Capt. Ogden far right…*

### Classmates

Before arriving at Company A, however, I met some classmates of mine from the Infantry Officers Basic Course and Airborne school at Fort Benning. Several had already been wounded, their heads wrapped in bandages. Some were on crutches, some had their arms in slings, but they seemed high-spirited. They were already veterans. They had seen action. I was just a novice. They told me that after you were wounded a second time you were reassigned in the base camp and didn't get field duty anymore. "Maybe, I thought to myself, I could just get a couple of light wounds, get awarded a Purple Heart, and wait it out until I went home".

My anxiety only increased as I listened to their war stories.

***Building up the Base Camp...***

Company A had a specified area of responsibility on the bunker line outpost. The bunker line was our perimeter of defense for the base camp. Other units were to our right and to our left.

Our company had begun to improve its portion of the base camp by building wood framed barracks. The tents and barracks were well back of the bunker line in what you might consider a "safe" zone. When I arrived we were still using tents but they were eventually upgraded.

I was assigned to a large tent with other officers. Three of us were rifle platoon leaders and one was a weapons platoon leader. The day I joined these officers became a day of transformation for me. I finally shared my fears with one of the other platoon leaders. Although he was sympathetic he was also very direct. He gave me a couple of Darvon tablets to help calm me down (placebo effect?) and then said, "Fred, there are forty men out there who are depending on you for their lives. It's not about you. It's about them! Get yourself together! Your job is to keep them alive. Embarrassed and humiliated, I was humbled beyond belief.

*Alpha company's living quarters…*

The other living quarters were for the enlisted men. These were squad size buildings that could accommodate 8-10 infantrymen. Platoon sergeants had their own facility. Our mess hall was a long tent before the upgrades.

During the monsoon season a tiny river-let ran right down the center. To my surprise the food was good and plentiful.

## Mail Call

It took several days before I received my first letter from home. Jan wrote to me every day. I did my best to do the same but it was not always possible because of our operations. Jan and I even used little tape recorders in order to hear each other's voices. It was so lovely to hear her voice. Letters from home were my emotional life line. I got occasional letters from my mom, dad or sister and some relatives and friends but, if I must be honest, Jan was the most faithful. This letter above was one of the last letters I had written to her, dated, May 13, 1967.

# VIETNAM – ONE SOLDIER'S EXPERIENCE

## Bunker Line under Attack

The very first night I was there, our portion of the bunker line came under heavy assault. The Viet Cong attacked us from the river in "sampans", small canoe-like boats. I had not been assigned any combat gear or weapon yet. The CO (commanding officer or XO, executive officer) I don't really remember who it was, asked me to carry a re-supply of ammo to the bunker line. The night was dark. I wasn't even sure where the bunker line was. I was given a few sketchy directions. I dutifully accepted my first combat order and I ran down the road until I saw what appeared to be bunkers made of sandbags silhouetted against the night sky.

I went into a bunker just to the right of the dirt road. Fortunately it was the correct one. I handed the ammo to someone and sat down with my back against the rear wall of sandbags. Tracer rounds were being fired to locate enemy targets. Grenades exploded and flares lit up the night sky to expose the VC approaching along the river. Support fire came from artillery and mortar rounds which exploded all around our position. I had a whole year to spend here and this was just the beginning. I hadn't yet been on a single operation or patrol. My real tests were yet to come.

## My Platoon

After a couple of days I was introduced to my platoon. I met Sergeant Terrian, my platoon sergeant. He was about age forty and in the latter years of his career. My four squad leaders were: Sergeant Sheffield (1st squad leader), Sergeant Zuck (2nd squad leader), Sergeant Belcher (3rd squad leader) and Sergeant Lewis (weapons squad leader). My radio operator's name was Specialist Harkleroad. My platoon was a mix of Hispanics, blacks and whites, an all-American platoon. There were forty-two of us in all, including my platoon sergeant and me. It consisted of four squads of ten men each, three rifle squads and one weapons squad which included two M60 machine gunners, assistant gunners and ammo bearers. On certain missions some men carried M-14's.

These were higher caliber weapons used to penetrate thick jungle and wooded areas. The rest carried M16 rifles which were lightweight, semi to fully automatic weapons. We also carried M79 grenade launchers, two in each rifle squad. That was quite a lot of firepower!

*Sergeant Terrian – center...*

## Bunker Line Duty

My first assignment with my platoon was bunker line duty. This was a relatively easy assignment unless we were under attack, of course. It was during these nights that I got better acquainted with my platoon sergeant. He was a Protestant and frequently read his bible. I, on the other hand, was Catholic and said my rosary. The bunker line was manned 24/7. Most of my assignments on the bunker line were at night.

Nights were a welcomed reprieve from the hot daytime sun. Sleeping rotation was two hours of sleep and then two hours of watch. I remember while trying to sleep large rats ran over my outstretched legs and feet. That was really creepy. I found it difficult to get to sleep. We all waited anxiously for the dawn.

Our bunker line outpost was called, Ann Margaret after the beautiful and sexy movie actress. It was a joke among the men that we would say we were sleeping on Ann Margaret. Phonetically over the radio, we called it *Alpha Mike.*

## Search and Destroy Operations

*Sgt. Lewis, facing front, consulting with Sgt. Belcher( right) and Sgt. Rodriguez ( left). Vietnamese villagers are gathered in the back-ground. This procedure was followed for the safety of the women, children and elderly.*

## Short Break from Work Detail

*Team leader c. - with his team...*

*Sgt. Zuck giving one of his team members a haircut...*

## My First Operation

The company commander, Captain Clay, decided that we would go on a small "sweep" around Ann Margaret and return to the base camp. The sweep, I think, was done mostly for my benefit. I believe the CO wanted to give me some field experience to see how I got on. We didn't run into any VC. I don't think the CO expected us to, really. It was what you might call a "walk in the park". There were lots of underbrush and woods though. I lost sight of my platoon almost as soon as we entered the woods but I managed to keep pace and we all returned safely. How will I be able to control the movement of my platoon when I can't even see them?

I gained more experience with each operation. I got to know my squad leaders better, how they worked and where they were positioned. We planned our formations in advance and changed them according to circumstances. Each squad leader was responsible to keep me within sight for my hand signals to stop, get down, change direction or change formation. This gave me better command and control. I became more confident and gradually I melded into the unit.

## Rite of Passage

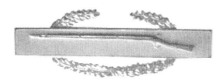

## Combat Infantryman's Badge

A coveted prize was the CIB, the Combat Infantryman's Badge. Only if you had engaged in live combat were you awarded the oak leaf cluster that surrounded the badge itself. My fellow officers each had one. I would have to earn mine.

My first encounter with the enemy was during a search and destroy mission. We were walking through a rubber tree plantation. We were well spread out as we walked into the plantation. Rubber trees are aligned in almost perfect rows.

Their canopy provided refreshing shade from the hot, burning Vietnam sun but except for the rubber trees we were basically exposed in the open space.

***Entering rubber tree plantation…***

It was beginning to look like another comfortable "walk in the park". Visibility was good all around. This also made us sitting ducks for being ambushed. This was uppermost on my mind as we moved deeper into and through the plantation. I could see that the plantation ended about 100 yards in front of us where it was bordered by heavy brush and undergrowth. My platoon was lead platoon that day. My gut instinct told me we were heading straight into an ambush. I signaled to my squad leaders. We all stopped and hit the ground in the prone position with our weapons trained on the wood line in front of us. I called the CO on the radio. My radio operator was always next to me or directly behind me. "Alpha 6, this is two six over." "This is Alpha Six over." "Request permission to Romeo by fire ". "Permission granted - out." Romeo stood for reconnaissance – a code word I used in case the VC could somehow hear or understand what we were about to do.

I remembered from one of our classes on reconnaissance that this was another technique to help locate the enemy. I ordered my squad leaders to fire a couple of rounds into the wood line to see if we got any response. After they fired five or six rounds we received a hail of small arms fire. A rifle grenade exploded a few feet to my left front just missing my head. If we had been standing up we would have taken casualties for sure. I was in my first firefight. The rest of the company was behind us. As lead platoon, it was our job to go on the offensive. We laid a heavy base of suppressing fire. I signaled one of my squads to spread out and circle right into the surrounding woods and to come at the VC from the right side. I went with the maneuvering squad. Hopefully the woods would keep our men less exposed as they moved in.

The flanking squad moved in quickly as we kept the rounds pouring in at the wood line in front of us. The VC stopped firing. I ordered a cease-fire. I didn't want to chance hitting our own men. The flanking squad was now well into the wood line closing in on the enemy.

I ordered the rest of the platoon forward and we continued our search for wounded or dead VC but found none. We discovered that they had been digging more trenches and tunnels. Apparently we had surprised a small element of VC or VC sympathizers.

I made a check with all the squad leaders and reported to the CO that we had sustained no casualties and everyone was present and accounted for. Maybe now I had earned my "CIB". I just wanted to be part of the team.

This first firefight and encounter with hostile fire was not what I expected. I still had visions of WWII. Great forces matched against great forces, John Wayne and Audie Murphy type stuff. This was different, very different. This was guerilla warfare.

Now you see them; now you don't. Mostly you don't see them. We were fighting against the Viet Cong or local sympathizers. They had no uniforms. Everyone looked the same.

It seemed everyone wore black pajamas. You could not distinguish between a local farmer from a Viet Cong. Maybe he was a farmer by day and an ambusher or sniper at night. Their tunnels, spider holes, booby traps and pungi pits were so well camouflaged. They worked as individuals or small groups of three or four. These are just a few of the reasons they were so successful.

During one operation we were receiving fire from a local village. We entered the village. Our interpreter, Kahn, questioned the villagers. He asked them where the firing was coming from. They answered that they knew nothing. They heard nothing. They saw nothing.

We searched the village and came up with only women, children and old men. As we walked away from the village the rounds started coming at us all over again. We knew whose side they were on. Or maybe it would be fairer to say they weren't on anyone's side, but just feared for their lives and wanted only to be left alone.

**My Promotion**

One night I was ordered to report to the company commander at battalion headquarters. When I entered I found there my company commander, along with other officers. I stood at attention, saluted and accepted my promotion to 1st Lieutenant on September 19, 1966. I was also awarded the coveted Combat Infantryman's Badge with Oak Leaf Cluster. This conferred upon me the distinction of having served my country in live combat against a hostile enemy. I finally felt accepted. I had proven myself under fire. It was a proud moment for me.

### Sniper up Front...

We were given another search and destroy mission. On this operation we were walking the edge of a wood line just inside a large clearing. The trees and undergrowth provided good, natural camouflage. We stayed clear of open terrain as much as possible. Again we were the lead platoon. We had not yet made enemy contact. This was the third morning we had taken this route. I had an uneasy sense that our luck was going to run out. Repeating the same pattern does not make for very good tactics.

I got a call on the radio from the CO to hold up and stay in place until another platoon from a different unit passed us up to take the lead. We took up defensive positions and waited. After a brief wait the other platoon walked through our position and took the lead. Not much time had passed when we heard shots fired at the front of the column. The rounds sounded like they came from a heavy caliber weapon.

*On the offensive but keep close to the wood-line...*

I received orders from the CO to secure a Landing Zone (LZ) for a medical evacuation. I guided the chopper down into a small clearing. The casualties were quickly loaded and flown away. One soldier had a severe stomach wound. His bloody hands were pressed against his belly. The medics had bandaged him up but the wound was serious and bleeding. The other soldier was the point man. I was told he was hit in the head with a 50 caliber round. I couldn't help thinking, "if we had not been ordered back that would have been two of my men – or me!"

***Transporting the wounded …***

*Placing the body bag respectfully on board the "chopper"...*

*Jets making their approach for bombing run ...*

After the wounded were cleared, an air strike was called in. Jets roared past our position dropping bombs. Huge pieces of shrapnel were flying through the trees from the explosions. As they whizzed by they tore off the bark and limbs of trees like a scissors through paper.

Large pieces of shrapnel went whistling by our heads. I signaled my squad leaders to have their men keep well low to the ground and to move away from the clearing. We moved deeper into the woods to avoid the flying debris. As we nudged forward the jets continued to drop their payload. We began to receive heavy small arms fire. We were now engaged with the enemy. Seeing them, however, was quite another thing.

Because we were now in contact with the VC, the pilots needed to know the left and right-most positions of our assault line. I had the last man in each of those positions drop a smoke grenade to give a clear indication of our location. Anything forward of that line of smoke would be bombed. Within seconds of dropping the smoke grenades, the planes came around. We could hear explosion after explosion. I was told these planes would be dropping napalm.

It seemed to me a very heavy assault. It was common tactics to find the enemy and then call close in fire support. With such close support there was always the risk of being hit by friendly fire.

Sometimes support came from jets, sometimes helicopter gunships and sometimes it was field artillery or mortars from our own weapons platoon.

I had no intelligence about the target. All I knew was that the enemy was there. We had two casualties and we were still receiving incoming fire. I never found out how many there were or how many we killed. After the bombing we moved forward to get an assessment and to continue our search for the VC. They had abandoned their position. The VC seemed to disappear into thin air. Did they take their wounded and dead with them or did we get anyone at all? This was going to be a tough war!

## Ambush Patrols

***Camouflaged and ready to lead my first ambush patrol...***

It wasn't long before I was given the opportunity to lead my first ambush patrol. Patrols were sent out every night and it wasn't uncommon to go out a couple of nights in a row. This caused some sleep deprivation because after coming in from patrol at four or five o'clock in the morning, the company very often had an operation planned for that same day.

My patrols consisted of ten or twelve men made up of two teams, Alpha and Bravo. It also included my RTO (radio/telephone operator) and a medic assigned to our patrol. Our medics were not only an invaluable resource by saving lives but they were loyal and highly dedicated to our mission. Because they were limited in numbers they were often out on patrols several nights in a row.

Sometimes we were assigned a scout dog team. This consisted of the dog and his handler. Scout dogs could pick up scent or movement at great distances. Each dog signaled his handler in a unique way. Sometimes a dog would perk up his ears, or sit up straight. Whatever the signal was, the handler could recognize it. On one patrol the dog signaled but it turned out to be a false alarm. It could have been a chicken or some other animal from the nearby village. I always felt a bit more confident having a scout dog along.

We prepared for the patrol with camouflage to darken our face, neck and hands. We wore soft hats, no helmets or flak jackets. We taped our dog tags so they would not shine or jangle together like a wind chime. The key element to our success was silence and the element of surprise under the cover of darkness. I made sure everyone knew his job and his position at the ambush site. I spelled it all out in the patrol order. I inspected each patrol to make sure we had enough ammo, flares, claymore mines and the right weapons. I questioned individuals in the patrol as to his specific role to be certain each man knew his responsibility. I made sure that those who were to carry mines had them and knew how to use them and exactly where they were to position them at the ambush site. One rehearsal and then we entered the darkness of night.

Our patrol passed through the bunker line. I coordinated with the command bunker as to what signal I would use upon our return. Most often it was a hand held flare such as a white or red five star cluster. This was critical to keep from getting shot upon re-entering the base camp. We also used a password to ensure identification of our patrol. Each patrol member needed to know that password.

The mission was to get to the ambush site undetected using stealth, silence and the element of surprise. The site selected was often a trail or intersecting trails that the VC used at night. Sometimes it was an area where there was known VC activity. We got into position in complete silence. Once the mines were set in place, that was the last thing – no one was to move. Anyone coming into our kill zone would trigger the ambush.

Now the waiting began. After some time we heard distinct footsteps and rustling in the bushes coming down along a trail which ran to the left of our ambush site. We were ready. I could feel the tension run throughout my whole body. But the trail ran parallel to our site.

Whatever or whoever it was continued on until their footsteps faded into the silence of the night. Patrols went out any time after dark. Most of mine were between 9:00 and 11:00 p.m. and returning at 4:00 or 5:00 a.m. Sitting still and in complete silence for several hours was difficult. During the monsoons the rain poured down soaking us to the skin. I liked setting out on patrol on rainy nights. Yes, we got soaked but the brush and twigs beneath our feet didn't crackle quite so loud, if at all. No noise was good noise. I also had it in the back of my mind that maybe the VC would take the night off and find a "honey" somewhere to spend the night.

Moonlit nights left us more vulnerable. The moonlight made it easier to find your way but you were an easy target for the Viet Cong. Mosquitoes by the hundreds bombarded our heads, neck and body. They mercilessly buzzed our ears. They so much craved to get on our skin. The insect repellent the Army provided really worked. It was oily but if you used enough of it, they kept off. The buzzing sound was maddening. If you had to pee you had to roll over sideways to relieve yourself without making any noise or unnecessary movement. Occasionally someone would cough or even try to smoke and hide it. Boy did that *piss* me off! Coughing, the smell of smoke, the lit end of a cigarette could be heard or seen for who knows how far in the night. I quit smoking myself when I got a smoker's cough. It's uncanny that someone would risk the lives of everyone for a lousy cigarette.

A couple of times I had to notify the CO that our position was compromised because of such infractions. I would give the CO my new coordinates and then move to that position and re-set the ambush. It was absolutely critical that the CO knew exactly where our patrol was on the map because the artillery would be firing rounds near or around our position. The last thing I wanted was for our own artillery to come raining down on our heads.

On one patrol, during my inspection, one of the men yelled out loud so the whole patrol could hear, "We're going to get our '*f***g*' asses killed out there". I asked the rest of the patrol if there was anyone else who felt that way. No one answered. I told this disruptive soldier to report immediately to the platoon sergeant. He was no longer in my patrol. We set out on our patrol with one less man. I hated to lose the firepower of even just one man but I could not tolerate anyone who might put the patrol at risk because of a bad attitude. Negativity can spread like *wild seed* and become the precursor to a sudden lack of concentration, confidence and resolve.

On another patrol, when daylight came, I found myself sitting on an unexploded 105 Howitzer round. We had arrived in our positions at night so I never saw it. As we cautiously started back to base camp we put a hand grenade on either side of the unexploded round. We tied a piece of cord to each grenade pin. We walked a good distance away, took cover by lying on the ground and pulled the pins out. What an explosion! It was live all right!

Nightly ambush patrols were a constant. We weaved our way silently into the darkness of night like snakes in the grass.

One night we came upon a "hooch" that was directly on our route to the ambush site. This caused me particular concern because there could be Viet Cong inside. Also, it could change the outcome of my patrol order due to an unanticipated response from the enemy. The patrol was manned and equipped to handle a specific, small objective. My men could become disorganized and confused if the enemy presented us with tactics we did not expect like being over- run by numbers, scattered, picked off or captured. We approached the hooch, encircling it, with great caution.

My suspicions were confirmed when we saw a shadowy figure silhouetted against the night sky running from the rear of the house. It would have been useless to pursue him. It was dark and we would never have found him much less hit a running target in the black of night. Nevertheless we went into the house and searched it. There was a young woman inside. It could have been her husband, a boyfriend or a VC whom we saw running. Who knows? But what struck me after we left is the fright we must have caused that young woman. My thoughts ran back to my own wife and how I would feel if a foreign army entered my house carrying automatic assault rifles.

What went through her mind? We left as quietly as we went in but she must have been trembling inside.

On another mission we spent nearly the entire night in an old woman's home. I used it as a headquarters from which to send out patrols. The old lady seemed friendly towards us. She made us hard-boiled eggs from her own chickens. Who can ever know what was in her heart. But our mission took priority. Their lives and life situations seemed almost irrelevant. We went where we willed and we didn't ask permission.

We had a mess sergeant who often, if not always, had a snack and hot coffee waiting for us in the mess tent after each patrol. As tired as we were or as soaked as we were we always stopped by in appreciation. We were relieved to be back in the base camp. Everyone accounted for!

## Thanksgiving Day

*This was our cook's Thanksgiving Day turkey for us.*

### Fire in the Officers' Tent

It had been a long night as we walked back to the base camp. We had been out on patrol once again. The hot coffee and snack, which the cook held for us, were welcome refreshment. The good news was that no operations were planned for early the next day. We could sleep late in the morning. How I welcomed that sleep.

I remember lying down on my bunk as the sun was rising higher in the sky but this was my time to sleep. Between our regular operations and frequent ambush patrols I was exhausted and in need of some good, uninterrupted rest. Sometime after I had fallen asleep I began to cough. The coughing got so bad that it had roused me from my deep slumber. I then began to choke. When I opened my eyes I discovered that the whole tent was filled with smoke. My eyes began to burn. I jumped up groping my way to the doorway. I yelled "fire fire", as I ran out.

When I was outside I looked back at the tent. There were no flames. Closer inspection revealed a yellow smoke grenade smoldering in the middle of the floor of the tent. There was no fire. I was relieved at that. Then, however, I was faced with the reality that someone must have placed the grenade in the tent while I was asleep. I surmised that whoever it was knew that I was in there alone. It was someone's idea of a practical joke or prank.

I looked all around but there was no one nearby. I felt rejected and excluded. I was now fighting not only one, but two enemies that I could not see.

## Frontal Assault

My platoon was taking up the rear. Our job was to protect the rear of the column and be ready to maneuver into position in case the lead platoon got pinned down. When I got the call from the "old man" (this is what we called our company commander) we were not directly taking fire ourselves. When I approached him, the entire company was pinned down in the woods taking heavy fire from the opposite side of a clearing. My orders from him were to attack and eliminate the enemy.

I returned to my squad leaders and gave them a quick operations order. We spread out and prepared for a frontal assault. Everyone was to move as fast as possible across the clearing, keeping as low to the ground as possible and to keep firing until we reached the wood line on the other side. The rest of the company would provide suppressing fires.

It sounded like a suicide mission to me. The clearing was about fifty to seventy–five yards of open terrain. On signal we hit the clearing blasting away at the opposite wood line. We moved in quickly, running and firing as we entered the woods. Just as in past experiences, when we got there we found no VC dead or wounded. Did we hit anybody? How can you win a war when you are so visible and your enemy seems to be invisible? I said a small prayer thanking God none of my men were hit. We searched around within the woods. We found nothing and returned to the company.

Just as we got back we started taking fire again. This time when we turned around we could see them. I spotted a couple of VC running along the edge of the wood line. I took a very good aim and fired two or three rounds. I saw one go down but did I hit him or did he dive for cover?

I began to have ambivalent feelings, relieved on the one hand that none of my men were killed or wounded, angry and frustrated that we had nothing to show for our efforts. I had reached the point of wanting to be able to say I had killed a Viet Cong. In the mean time the company was moving on. It was time to go. It seemed to me that we were doing a lot of finding but not much killing.

## Air Assault

Before each operation we received a detailed operations order from the company commander. It was up to my platoon sergeant and squad leaders to ensure that the platoon was at the landing zone on time with all the right equipment. I met them on the LZ. Sometimes it was hurry up and wait. We were always ready.

*Lt. Voto and Sgt. Zuck (standing) waiting for choppers to arrive...*

I constantly questioned myself, " Have I missed or forgotten something critical to our mission?" Also running through my mind was: "Will we all make it back?" I was very protective of my men by this time. I had set a very high standard. Even one wounded was not acceptable to me. Maybe that was unrealistic but I just could not settle for anything less.

When the choppers flew in they were just little specs in the distant sky. As they came closer you could hear that classic Huey sound of the rotors. A rush of adrenalin always came over me.

*Here they come!  There's no turning back now!*
*"The chase is on…"*

Even though I had no idea what we would face it was always an awesome sight. Each team jumped in and we were airborne in seconds. The doors were wide open and the door gunners were in their positions with their machine guns always at the ready.

The cool breezes felt good against our perspiration soaked fatigues. It was an incredible way to fight the enemy. Now you don't see us, now you do! It gave us great mobility and the element of surprise.

If the flight was long my mind would drift off to home, to Jan and Michelle. Here I was speeding through the air at treetop level over rice paddies and jungles ready to drop deep into Viet Cong territory. Where were they at this very same moment? Could I keep myself alive to see them again? I looked around the chopper at the young faces. Sometimes the men joked and laughed but their faces grew serious and tense as we got closer to the enemy LZ.

We could see the helicopter gunships going in first firing their rockets. Then the door gunners began firing, blasting the wood line. In a few dramatic seconds we were on the ground running and firing into the woods. We were receiving small arms fire. The choppers seemed to be still moving when we jumped out.

***Chopper next to us in formation ...***

They weren't sticking around! There was too much fire coming from the wood line. The landing zone was an open rice paddy and my machine gunner was stuck knee deep in mud. I reached back with my rifle butt. He grabbed hold and I just pulled until he was free. We kept firing at the wood line as we moved forward. The VC had gone because we got in with a lot of firepower. Thank God for the helicopter gunships which strafed the woods just before we hit the ground?  Once again there were no dead VC, there were no wounded.  I seriously began to doubt we could win this war.  You can't kill what you can't see.

**Fire Superiority – Another Frontal Assault**

We had been on a search and destroy mission when I got a call from the CO that he had come under heavy enemy fire.

My platoon was at a distance so we were not involved in the initial contact. As we drew closer to the rest of the company we could hear small arms fire. The CO ordered me to take out the enemy by assaulting the wood line from where they were receiving fire.

My plan of attack was to leave one squad behind. To our right was slightly higher terrain. It was perfect for a machine gunner to lay down suppressing fire in support of our assault. Once we masked their fire they were to join the rest of us in continuing the assault into the wood line.

I took the rest of the platoon, including the other machine gunner with me. My squad leaders didn't need much direction and we fanned out in a line for the assault.

I wanted good distance between each man so that we would appear to the enemy as a superior force. It would also provide enough distance to minimize casualties from rifle grenades or booby traps. The predetermined signal to launch our attack was that I would fire the first round when we were ready.

Once that shot was fired, the covering squad was to commence firing, very heavy fire into the objective until they ran the risk of hitting us as we crossed.

It was like clockwork. I fired the first round and I could hear a barrage of fire coming from the other squad. Hopefully that would keep the enemy down so that the rest of us could advance quickly on their position. But suddenly things started to go wrong.

We were taking heavy small arms fire still and my machine gunner began to slow down. Next he was down on one knee and he had stopped firing. I said to myself, "God, not now"! I could see that we were losing momentum fast. This was a death sentence for sure. I ran up behind him and kicked him with my boot. I grabbed him by his shirt. I pulled and pushed him to get on his feet again.

I remember screaming, "Get the "f…" up and keep firing." Shocked at my language and my aggressiveness, he got up and began firing. It wasn't in my nature to be vulgar or to be cursing. I think that because it was so out of character for me that this had a shock effect. It was the right moment for me to be different.

We regained the ground we had lost and caught up with the rest of the assault line. I checked up and down the line. I yelled and barked out orders. I moved left and right to keep the line straight and to keep the assault moving forward. If either end of the line fell back the assault would weaken. I could see that the men were responding.

They were moving forward quickly and keeping a straight line. We had regained our momentum.

During our basic officer training we were told that it was not uncommon for men during an assault to slow down, stop or even get down and freeze. It was my job to make sure this didn't happen. Our lives depended on it.

We hit the wood line firing and then quickly spread out. We went deeper into the woods, left and right to find the VC. Nothing! The assault was over. I checked for a count. I received reports from my squad leaders. All were present and accounted for.

But where were the VC? How could we have taken so much fire; launched a heavy assault and come up with zero. Did it really happen? I assure you it did. This war was really starting to frustrate me. I wanted results. I wanted to win. I thought that was what we came here to do, to win!

In a hot firefight, it doesn't take long to expend ammunition. A re-supply of ammo had already been ordered. The chopper arrived and dumped a box of grenades and extra ammunition but it was too late. The firefight was over. The rest of the company had already started to move out so we carried as much as we could of the extra ammunition and left a gift from Uncle Sam to the VC. It happens!

## Almost Cut Off

***RTO, Specialist Harkleroad, on search and destroy mission…***

My platoon was taking up the rear just after we had another encounter with the VC. As a result of the encounter my men were spread out. I wanted to be sure that we left no one behind so my RTO and I made our way back to the rear. Once we confirmed that we had everyone, the two of us walked through the rice paddy that was adjacent to the wood line. We were crossing over a dyke when shots were fired directly at us. I heard one round go whizzing by my left ear. We did a somersault backward into the muddy rice paddy. When we poked our heads up to see where the firing was coming from another round hit my RTO.

I thought Harkleroad had been hit directly in the face but what had happened was the round hit directly in front of his face and embedded itself in the mud.   With mud all over his face he grinned at me.  We laid low beneath the dyke.  That was the only cover we had.  My M16 was full of mud.  I was concerned that it would jam. To test it I fired a single shot in the direction that I thought the rounds had come from.  My M16 worked fine! We were fired at a couple more times but we kept our heads low and began to belly crawl along the dyke.  I radioed the old man, "Alpha six, this is two six over". "This is Alpha Six, over."  "We're pinned down and taking rounds back here, over."  "There's nobody shooting.  Get up here!  Over and out!"

We knew that we had been cut off and we didn't expect anyone to come back to help us.  The rest of the company was moving on.  My RTO and I looked at each other with a grin on our faces that said to each other, "Yeah, right!"  We crawled to within twenty yards or so of the woods and made a run for it.  We were in and quickly caught up to our platoon.

## Chapel at Base Camp

## Father Jared, saying Mass...

Mass was something I missed and really hungered for. A chapel had been built not too far from our company area. A young priest, Fr. Jared, said Mass for us. It wasn't often that I was in the base camp. When I was there on a Sunday, I looked forward to the quiet and peacefulness of the Mass, especially the Eucharist. I assisted at Mass by serving as altar boy. I was an altar boy as a child growing up in Boston. Sometimes I brought a couple of enlisted men with me.

There for a brief time, we could just be Christians together. Occasionally, in the evening I also said the rosary at the chapel. I invited others to come. We had a small but dedicated and enthusiastic group for the rosary. I was pleased to lead them in this devotion. I remember the contentment I had after serving Mass or praying the rosary. Fear and anxiety seemed far off during those brief moments of solace.

## Phu Hoa Dong

I also accompanied the priest by helicopter to say Mass for the people at Phu Hoa Dong, a tiny village just north of our base camp. It was a very short distance by chopper. The bells were always ringing in the small church as the chopper landed in a nearby field. It was like calling out to the VC, "Here I am!" I took my M16 with me, even into the church. This may seem sacrilegious but I was on my own and out of the base camp. Once I was issued my M16, I never went anywhere without it. Why we were not ambushed, I'll never know. But only the local villagers came. I found the Vietnamese of that village so welcoming and grateful. I believe that God was with us during those times.

Catholics were not encouraged to read the Bible like our protestant brethren. I didn't have a Bible. I was fortunate to meet Reverend Bobby Moore later in "Rach Kien" who kindly gave me an inscribed copy. It has been a gift I have treasured to this day.

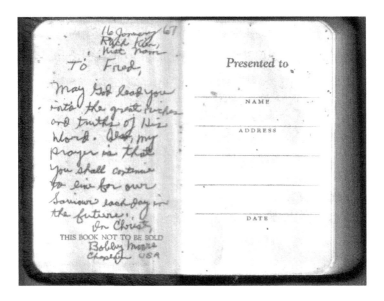

**Gift from Reverend Bobby Moore...**

**Military Justice**

One day I received unexpected orders. They read that on such and such a date at such and such a time I was to act as prosecuting officer in a case involving an enlisted man charged with negligent homicide of a 12 year old Vietnamese boy. Military Officers could be assigned to legal cases as prosecutors which was an integral part of the Military Justice System.

My mind began racing as I tried to remember what I had learned about the Uniform Code of Military Justice. I wasn't an attorney. The defendant had an officer from the Judge Advocates Corp who was a graduate of law school and a bona fide attorney. I had to prepare myself. I got onto the chopper especially provided for me and I was flown to the area where this court martial was to take place. This was to be a Special Court Martial. It was comprised of three officers as judges and these three officers would determine the fate of the accused. I represented the prosecution and the previously referred to attorney was his defense lawyer.

My first task was to visit the CID, the Criminal Investigation Division. They held the file on this case. The file contained all the applicable documents and photographs. I'm sure they could see my lack of experience. This was my first case in Military Justice. They apprised me of the "elements of proof" which had to be presented to the Special Court in order to prove that the accused was guilty of the allegation, namely, "negligent homicide". I took the file and read all the material, the charges, the circumstances and all the details pertaining to the case. The main elements of proof as I recall were:

1. There was in fact a dead person.
2. That the accused was indeed negligent resulting in the death of the victim.

The file contained explicit and very graphic photos of the victim. The difficulty was to prove negligence. I was taken aback by the photo of this young boy lying on the ground, his head lying in a pool of blood. His dead body, his mother, his family, his friends all seemed to be crying out to me, "*guilty, guilty!*" But was the defendant guilty? That remained to be seen.

The background was that the victim was scavenging among what I understood to be a laterite pit or dump pile. The children came to this spot to scavenge for articles they could use or sell. This young victim was among them. The defendant was on guard duty. The incident occurred at night. It was apparently customary for the guards to fire rounds in the air to frighten the children away.

When the case opened I demonstrated to the judges that indeed there was a dead person as evidenced by the photograph taken by the CID. I entered this as evidence. The defending attorney remained silent.

Proving negligence presented a greater challenge. My strategy was to demonstrate to the presiding officers that the defendant was well aware and well trained about weapon safety. I began by asking him to describe in his own words what happened that night.

He told the court that in order to frighten the kids away he fired his weapon at the embankment in front of him. He went on to say that the bullet must have ricocheted and hit the child.

I proceeded to ask the defendant if he had ever heard of the phrase, "Keep your weapon up and down range". He replied in the affirmative. I asked him if he knew why he was taught this.

He answered, "For safety so as not to hit anyone by accident."

I then asked him if anyone else was firing at the time of the incident. He answered "no". "So you were the only one who fired, is that correct?" I asked. He answered, "Yes". I then asked him if there was any doubt in his mind that it was his round that hit the child. He answered, "No". At this juncture the defending attorney said a few words on his client's behalf. I didn't think anything he said discredited in any way the evidence I had presented thus far.

In my final argument, I told the presiding officers that he has admitted himself that it was his weapon that fired the fatal round. He was trained to fire into the air. Clearly this man was negligent in the dispensation of his duties which cost the life of an innocent 12-year-old boy. I recommended that the defendant, therefore, be found guilty of negligent homicide.

The court adjourned for the day. I was provided a place to sleep. I was up early the next morning to hear the verdict. The defendant had been in country an extra two months awaiting this trial. His tour of duty had already been completed. We entered the room. The presiding officers came in and sat down before us.

The verdict was quickly read, **NOT GUILTY!**

I couldn't believe that they could come up with a not guilty verdict but there it was. He was now free to leave the country and go home. I quarreled within myself. Did they just want to let him go home? He spent two extra months in country awaiting trial. Was it because they just were not going to convict him regardless? Was it because my feelings were hurt that I didn't win?

It was dark. It was not intentional. Maybe it was just what the military calls, "collateral damage". I had no answers. It was over. I had fulfilled my duty and obligation. As I pondered these events, the chopper picked me up and flew me back to my platoon, to more familiar territory. I was not a lawyer. I was a rifle platoon leader.

## Pay Officer

In addition to our primary duty, officers were also assigned ancillary duties as well. One of these duties was that of payroll officer. I was assigned a .45-caliber pistol and I was responsible to pay the enlisted men. Each soldier signed a receipt that he had been paid the correct amount. I had never been payroll officer so I needed some coaching from my peers. It wasn't complicated but I just needed some guidelines as to how to go about the task. I don't exactly recall what base camp I was assigned to in order to exercise my duties as pay officer but we had to fly to the destination. Several other officers were also assigned to the same duty and we were airlifted to the base camp. I made my rounds. I paid everyone and got signed receipts.

I recall it was a very hot day - dry and dusty. All the pay officers met at a rendezvous point located next to a nearby officers' club and awaited the Caribou which was to fly us back to Cu Chi.

We all boarded the aircraft and took our seats opposite one another. There was one row on each side of the aircraft. The pilot turned up the engines and as they roared we took off down the runway. It seemed to me to be a makeshift sort of runway, rather short. There was a big drop off at the end of the runway which I noticed as the aircraft lifted itself into the air. The plane climbed steadily banking left as we gained altitude. We were all chatting a bit. Some of us knew each other and others were getting to know one another. It was the usual stuff, what unit are you with and other such small talk.

Suddenly we heard a big crunching, grinding sound on the right hand side of the aircraft. I looked out the small portal window and I could see that the right engine had ground to a complete halt. The propeller was jammed! The aircraft immediately began to lose altitude. Who would have thought this would be our fate? We would die, not in a heroic firefight but in a crashing Caribou. We all tightened our steel helmet straps under our chins and braced ourselves one against the other. The faces across from me were frozen in the moment as though they were chiseled in stone. Everyone was silent.

We just waited. I looked out the small window over my left shoulder and could see the treetops. In only seconds we would crash headlong into the jungle below. But we never hit the treetops. Suddenly the tarmac re-appeared. The aircraft hit the runway on the opposite end from which we had taken off. While we were waiting for the aircraft to crash the pilot had apparently gained enough altitude to turn back to the opposite end of the runway and land on the tarmac. When he reversed engines the aircraft turned sideways. We slid to a stop just before the big drop off. It was a miracle! We were safe. We got out of the aircraft in a hurry.

A new engine or engine parts were ordered. We had to stay a day or two until the aircraft was repaired. We all praised and thanked the pilot for saving our lives. We bought him drink after drink, far more than he could handle. Once repairs were completed, we flew out without incident. It was good to be back in Cu Chi.

On another flight in a Caribou, the pilot could not get the landing gears to go down. Finally, after four failed attempts the landing gears responded and we landed safely. I was never really afraid of flying but these two experiences dulled my enthusiasm for Caribous.

## Pay Officer a Second Time

I had pay officer duty a second time. This time I was to pay the enlisted men in the field hospital. I was approaching the hospital when a jeep pulled up just in front of me to my left.

I did not recognize the insignia patch of the passenger but I knew it was not a combat insignia. The passenger was in fatigues and his back was soaked with perspiration. As he got out of the jeep he turned in my direction so that we were facing each other.

He looked familiar to me. He was very tall with broad shoulders. He addressed me by reading my nametag, which was sewn on the front of my fatigues. "Voto, Lieutenant Voto, Hi, my name is James Garner." Shocked, to say the least, I said, "Hello, pleased to meet you sir!" We shook hands. I thanked him for coming to visit. It was a fleeting, chance meeting but I admired the star for his role in the *Maverick* TV series. I had watched him many times at home on television. I was very impressed that he would come all the way to Vietnam to visit our wounded soldiers.

**Field Hospital**

I had spent so much time on the line that I never got an opportunity to come this far back in the base camp to visit the hospital ward. I had seen a few men that had been wounded in firefights out in the field. I thought I knew what to expect. I had been lucky so far. I hadn't lost a man nor had anyone in my platoon been wounded.

I finished my duties as quickly as possible. I paid the men and got signatures from those who were able to sign. I was not on my own as far as my time was concerned. I had to complete my assignment and return immediately to the Company area. I did, however, spend some time talking to the wounded. I spoke to the nurses, asking about each patient and how he was doing. Their wounds were much more severe than I could have imagined. I wished them well.

My words seemed so shallow in light of what they had to endure. Some I knew would not survive. This gave me pause to wonder, so much injury, so much suffering – these are just kids!

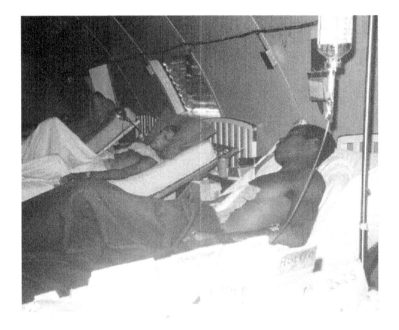

**Visiting our wounded ...**

The sun was setting, fading from yellow to orange as I made my way back to the Company. My mood was somber and my soul was no longer at peace.

## Officers' Club

There was an ongoing effort to make life a little more comfortable for the enlisted men. Work was underway to build an NCO club. After the enlisted men's club was finished then the officer's club was built. The inside of the officer's club had the atmosphere of some tropical bar, probably because the 25th Division was from Hawaii. There were several sets of tables and chairs. An NCO tended the bar for us. Drinks were cheap and, needless to say, we generously indulged ourselves. We were not in the base camp often so it was a treat to have some beer or gin and tonics. That's what we were drinking this particular night, gin and tonics.

I had by this time graduated to living in a hex tent with one other officer. It was almost like having your own room. It was better than living in the larger tent with three other officers. I asked an African-American officer, Lieutenant Thomas, to be my roommate. He had just arrived. He was sharp in appearance and was as gung-ho as any other officers I had met. We had gotten along well after our first meeting so I thought we would make good roommates.

One night my new roommate and I were at the officers' club sitting at a table together. Father Pete, our newly assigned Catholic priest was also there. A few other officers were there as well. I do not recollect how things got started but my roommate got into a heated exchange of words with an officer at another table. This other officer had been relieved of combat duty during the initial assaults on the Division prior to my arrival. I was not about to judge the merits of anyone in combat. Shock, fear and trauma can be crippling. Given the same set of circumstances how might anyone react?

Racial slurs soon began to fly between these two. They obviously had an issue between them about which I was unaware. The argument escalated quickly. I automatically looked to Father Pete to quell the situation. My childhood experience was that priests could always bring calm and peace to any situation, or so I believed. How naïve I was. I watched Father Pete remove himself from the club by quietly walking out the door. I pass no judgment on the good father.

It was my own immaturity to expect him to get involved. It was up to me to stop this before someone got hurt. Both men were now on their feet. I grabbed my roommate and literally pushed him out the door and walked him quickly to our tent. We were both a bit intoxicated. Otherwise maybe none of this would have happened.

He sat on his bunk and I sat on mine as he began to tell me of his lifetime experience of prejudices against "niggers". I asked him how it was that he and I got on so well. We didn't seem to have a problem. He answered that I was different. I wasn't a racist like most whites he had known. His story was a sad one. I listened to all the injustices he had endured growing up. "Even in the Army, there is racism", he said. We talked late into the night. We both had to be up early the next morning. I told him how sorry I was for all his pain and assured him he could trust me to be his friend.

### *Tay Ninh*

**Building bunkers for the 196th Light Infantry Brigade...**

Our company received orders for Tay Ninh. Tay Ninh was located about twenty miles from Cu Chi, maybe about fifty-five miles northwest of Saigon. Our mission was to set up and fortify a base camp for the incoming 196th Light Infantry Brigade. We were responsible for a certain sector and began the daunting task of filling hundreds of sandbags for making bunkers. This would be the main line of defense. The work was hot, dry and slow. The enlisted men worked tirelessly to get things ready. We were not exactly sure when the unit would arrive. It was our job to ensure that they had a strong defensive position when they did arrive. Until the bunkers were built we used our ponchos as tents. However, if we were outside the perimeter, we slept in one-man foxholes. They were no more than shallow ditches dug deep enough and long enough to fit a body.

This offered at least some minimal protection from shrapnel in case we came under attack from mortars or other explosives such as rifle grenades. One night it poured rain and the ditch just filled with water. I basically lay in a puddle of water the whole night. Morning could not come soon enough.

The men built bunkers by day and then most nights we sent out ambush patrols. I sent out "Listening Posts", or "LPs", made up of three or four men, including one NCO with a radio. Because of their small number they were not sent out too far, but far enough to give early warning of an approaching enemy. Only if necessary would they engage the enemy otherwise they were to work their way back to our re-enforced positions. We never sent men out to be sacrificed. It was a necessary assignment and a dangerous one but we weren't looking to make dead heroes. Each LP reported back to me every half hour or so. One night an LP called on the radio that they were receiving fire. They gave me the position of the enemy as best they could determine. I decided to call in a Fire Mission. I gave exact map coordinates. This should have brought the artillery rounds right on top of the VC within 10 meters. In came the rounds.

The LP leader radioed back to me that we had successfully bracketed the target. I gave the order to "fire for effect". After a few rounds exploded the LP ran back in. It was too close.

No two rounds will fall in the exact same spot or area. Apparently one exploded off target. One of my men showed me that a piece of shrapnel had cut off the butt end of his M16.

Despite the close call, they set out after a little while to establish a new LP. The heavy barrage of artillery must have given the VC second thoughts as well. Except for the night ambush patrols, which were frequent, duty at Tay Ninh was not so bad.

We went on some search and destroy missions but again, our main responsibility was to prepare the base camp. When the Brigade finally arrived we handed over responsibility.

There was a geological phenomenon at Tay Ninh that was also very unique. Out of the flat earth rose a giant called Nui Bah Dinh or "Black Virgin Mountain". It was visible from the ground but from the air it was majestic.

*Nui Bah Din – "Black Virgin Mountain"…*

## Memorial Service

A late afternoon memorial service was held for our fallen soldiers.
I do not know who they were or from what unit they belonged.
I had a lot of marching experience having been on the drill team in
college so I wanted my platoon to look sharp. It was the only
tribute we could make to those who had sacrificed their lives.

We marched into the bright setting sun to our designated position.
To our front and slightly to the left stood several M16s with
bayonets stuck into the earth. The helmets of the fallen soldiers
rested lifelessly on the butt end of the rifle. The chaplain prayed
for God's favor and mercy upon these brave young souls.

There was a moment of silence. The intense silence was broken
with the melancholy and plaintiff sound of taps. The taps
continued their languid, plaintiff melody. I fought back the tears
that began to well up in my eyes. I did not know these men but
they were my brothers in arms. This was a sad moment.

My thoughts wandered to their loved ones at home.
How heartbroken they will be when they get the news.
Then orders were given to commence our march back to our
respective areas. It is a vision I shall never forget.

## Trip to Cu Chi – A Day Off

As I had mentioned I was married and a Catholic. Adultery and infidelity, therefore, were to be avoided. I did not want to break my fidelity to Jan. Many of the enlisted men and officers found their way to downtown Cu Chi for reasons that do not need elaboration. We were all living with few pleasures. The pleasure of being with a woman was for many irresistible. I was often invited and sometimes teased by one particular Chief Warrant Officer.

He wanted me to go to Cu Chi to have a good time and relax a bit. I had always refused but I must admit that I was curious. I was keenly aware of my commitment to my wife, Jan. I was confident that I would not be cajoled into participating.

Pleased that I was going, we went off in a jeep to downtown Cu Chi. I was fascinated by the culture I saw, notwithstanding the rows and rows of tin huts, which had by now become a local industry.

The town of Cu Chi was quite colorful with quaint shops and clothes made from silk, silk paintings and sundry items for purchase by the Americans. There was a laundry, a barbershop and other small retail shops.

I bought a lovely, pink (and expensive by Vietnamese standards), top and bottom set from one of these shops for a little girl who was riding her tricycle nearby. She looked poor and so I told the owner that the outfit was for this little girl. I purchased the item for her but for all I knew the child could have been the shop owner's daughter.

***Big sister with baby brother in tow ...***

### *The Ambush – Cu Chi...*

Most of my pay went directly home but even the few dollars I took for myself each month just stayed in my pocket. There was no place to spend it unless you went to Cu Chi town and that was something I did only this once.

My friends in the meantime had gone into this room which I immediately recognized as the place where it all happened. An older woman greeted me. She was "*the Madam*". I didn't really have any experience in these things. Then a young woman came over and sat on my lap. She ordered a Saigon Tea from the Madam. My friends were smiling to see how I was reacting to all this. There were back rooms with curtains and a few men engaged in some heavy petting sitting in various parts of the room I was in. I presumed they were waiting their turn. In the meantime my friend just kept giving me the high sign, so to speak and smiling at me all the time. It seemed to amuse him that I was there.

After two or three of these expensive "teas", I gathered my emotional strength and told my friend I would be waiting outside. Dumped from my lap the young girl had a very confused look on her face. I don't know how I would have fared if the young girl, and I say girl, because they were probably only sixteen or so, had been particularly attractive. As it was she was rather ugly. I had tested my willpower far enough. I got up and walked out into the bright sunshine.

I fulfilled my promise to go to Cu Chi with my friend. He was just looking for me to let my hair down a bit. When he re-appeared we hopped into the jeep and headed back to the base camp. I had gone to downtown Cu Chi. There was no more teasing after that. I could now put this *almost* misadventure behind me.

## Operation Attleboro

Of all the operations in which I participated, none were of the size and magnitude of Operation Attleboro. There was an interesting prelude to this operation from my personal point of view. I had been given an operations order from the company commander. I knew nothing about Operation Attleboro at the time. The order was to be a three day, platoon size search and destroy mission.

I was apprehensive and particularly concerned about this mission. I was to lead my platoon, the 2nd platoon, on a three day search and destroy mission through the infamous Hobo Woods. I had been told more than one story about the infestation of Viet Cong in that area. It was a Viet Cong stronghold. If we got into trouble we would be completely on our own.

The Hobo Woods was just north, northwest of our base camp in Cu Chi. This was the area where the Wolfhounds had encountered many VC with heavy losses to both sides. The success of this operation to a large extent depended on our logistics as well as our execution. There was a river crossing involved which I felt would make us vulnerable and a potentially easy target.

It would require rope and other items that we would not ordinarily carry on a normal operation. Extra ammo, smoke and hand grenades would have to be taken which would increase the load that each soldier had to carry. We also would take 60mm mortars in order to have additional firepower. We had to provide food for three days and maybe a bit more in case our operation was unexpectedly extended. We were to be flown in by chopper and in three days the choppers would lift us out. The execution and logistics parts of the operations order contained much more detail than I had ever prepared. We had a strong swimmer in our platoon who volunteered to swim across the river with the rope and the rest would then follow using the rope as a guide and support. It all sounded like very risky business and would certainly test my personal skills. After giving my NCO's a brief warning order I went off to write my operations order.

I was writing this lengthy operations order while sitting in front of one of the enlisted men's tents where there was some cool shade. Sergeant Terrian came over to me. "Sir, he said, the mission has been scrapped, get your gear and meet us on the landing zone in five minutes. We're going to participate in a huge multi-force operation called, Operation Attleboro."

In five minutes I had my gear and I was on the landing zone. The platoon was broken up into teams and ready to board the choppers. I never saw the landing zone so full of troops. Within minutes I could see little specs in the sky off in the distance. The black specs grew larger and larger as they approached. It was an amazing sight as helicopter after helicopter touched down for a split second and almost instantly was airborne again.

After we landed the CO gave the platoon leaders a quick briefing. We were participants in what was called a "hammer and anvil" operation. Our company was to be part of the anvil.

This was a multi-divisional operation and soldiers from other divisions were to drive the enemy "the hammer" into our awaiting ambush "the anvil".

I recall passing through and meeting men from the 173rd Airborne, the Big Red One, the 4th Division, the Ninth Division and the Aussies with their distinctive "bush" hats.

*Incoming choppers…*

*My radio operator waiting for order to move out…*

*A little rest before the order comes to board choppers...*

***Operation Attleboro assembly area…***

At last we were going to get the VC! I was waiting for a moment like this when we could really make a difference in this war.

After landing we moved to our designated forward position. We camouflaged ourselves and now it was just a matter of waiting for the Viet Cong to come running into our trap. I could feel the tension as we waited quietly in ambush.

We were in place for some time when I heard an explosion. It sounded like a grenade. Finally our moment had arrived. After a few minutes I heard some chatter on the radio. As I listened I could hear my CO talking to one of the other platoon leaders in our company. The platoon leader informed the CO that his platoon sergeant was down. The CO asked if he was WIA (wounded in action) or KIA, (killed in action). The dreaded words came back, "Kilo, India, Alpha".

I was stunned. I had been just recently laughing and chatting with him. He was an older "salty" NCO. He was fond of sardines in tomato sauce. He bought these items so that he could eat them instead of the much-maligned C-rations. He even had a bottle of whiskey with him and we shared a drink together. Dead! He was dead! In an instant, a jovial and good natured career soldier was dead. The question remained, "How did it happen?"

Word crept its way up the line and this is what I was told. He was fond of souvenirs and went into nearby hooch. Two VC saw that he was alone. They took him by surprise, slit his throat and placed a hand grenade under his body.

That explained the explosion I heard. My grief at hearing this grew deeper and then it turned into anger. I wanted now more than ever to kill some VC. Maybe a little longer wait and I would have my chance. But my chance never came. The enemy had been driven in the wrong direction. All this turned to nothing and so we moved out and set up a large perimeter of defense with companies from other divisions. We had to make sure there were no gaps in the perimeter of defense between units. Each man on the end of our line had to make physical contact with the man to his right or left. Fire sectors which overlapped were established to be sure that the entire area was covered in case of an assault or infiltration. Now it was more waiting. Nothing was happening! I was totally frustrated and disappointed with our commanders for not having pulled off this so-called "hammer and anvil" plan.

Coordination of the perimeter was complete before nightfall. After dark anything that moved in front of that line was considered an enemy target. The claymore mines had to be placed out in front and the wire with the trigger carried back to the perimeter. We sat waiting as twilight fell on our position and the mosquitoes began their nightly raid on our flesh. I did not know the full scale of the operation. We just did what we were told and followed orders.

It was just about twilight, that moment when darkness sweeps away all remnants of the day. Suddenly I heard a rip of automatic fire that pierced the evening silence. It seemed like automatic fire to me, *"tat, tat, tat"*. Were we under attack? Everything went silent again.

We stayed on alert and at the ready for oncoming VC. But none came. What came instead was more bad news. Someone from another unit had been killed by friendly fire. Apparently, without notifying the man to his right and his left, which was the protocol, one of our soldiers walked out in front of the line to adjust his claymore mine. Mistaken for the enemy he was killed. What a waste! We had shot one of our own. I couldn't believe it! This added to the growing pain within me of another precious life lost. It caused me bitter anguish. I didn't even know the soldier! It didn't matter. What mattered was that another family would hear the tragic and dreaded news that their son, brother or husband was killed in action.

**The Doctor**

It was a hot, dry day in the base camp. I had the pleasure of meeting a new young physician assigned to our battalion. He was of a quiet disposition and we had a few things in common we could talk about. We had some spare time on this particular morning and agreed to meet in the mess tent and have a cup of coffee together. The tent was situated on high ground above a slight embankment or hillside. I welcomed this brief respite from my regular duties.

We were in the midst of our conversation when the silence of this sleepy sunny morning was broken by the sound of a single gunshot. It sounded to me like a .45 caliber weapon which some officers carried. I jumped up and ran in the direction from which the shot was fired, the doctor following in quick pursuit.

There was a small clump of trees that was growing on the edge of a slight dip in the terrain at the bottom of this embankment. The shot sounded like it came from there. When we arrived we found the reconnaissance platoon leader lying in a vast pool of blood. The condition of his head would be too graphic to describe.

The doctor realized immediately that he could not even try a tracheotomy as a lifesaving measure. The doctor had only been with us a brief time and had not yet seen many battle wounds. There was nothing he could do for him. The lieutenant was dead! The doctor was visibly shaken. Although I did not know this officer well, I did know him. I knew him well enough that he had confided in me that he had received a "Dear John" letter from his girlfriend a few days earlier.

I had suggested to him that perhaps he could take a couple days off and I would lead his reconnaissance platoon on the next operation. He thanked me but refused. He said, "I'll be alright".

Within a few days there was an investigation of the incident. To my surprise I was told that his father was a Colonel stationed in Thailand. After his arrival his father, along with the investigators reviewed the area. Together they continued their investigation. The doctor and I had already reported to our superiors what we heard and how the doctor and I had responded.

In the final analysis, it was determined to be an accidental shooting while he was cleaning his weapon. This conclusion remained suspect to me, both because of the knowledge I had about the "Dear John" letter and the fact that this officer was well trained. Surely he would have cleared his weapon before attempting to clean it. He had also said something else which I cannot reveal lest there be any flaw in my memory of the details leading up to this tragic incident. . I accepted the findings of the investigation that it was an accidental death because I saw no gain to suggest otherwise. The answer as to what really happened on that hot, dry sunny day lies buried with this dedicated reconnaissance platoon leader.

**Rounding Up the Villagers**

In order to find the men in the village that were VC or VC sympathizers, we had to round up the women and children in a central area in an open rice paddy. It was for their safety and also for our protection. Women could be communicators of our location and our activities as well as acting as spies for the VC. Their husbands or brothers could be VC. We never knew if a village was friendly or not.

***Local Vietnamese women and children...***

I found this part of our duties distasteful. A helicopter would circle above the village. An interpreter, using a hand held amplifier, would tell all the women and children of the village to come to the field. I thought of my own wife and child and how

I would hate anyone to do to them what we were doing to these women and children. Mothers with babies suckling at their breasts, frightened little children huddled together and squatting in an open sun baked field. I understood on one level that it was necessary. On another level, I found this to be very degrading. I couldn't reconcile this within myself. What they did not know was that we had a strict policy to avoid at all cost any injury to the local population. So much so was this policy carried out that we ourselves were put at risk. I had to request permission from the company commander in order to return fire, despite the fact that we were clearly being fired upon.

## A Welcomed Rest

We had been out for about six or seven days on a search and destroy mission. We were exhausted for lack of sleep. Daily we sent out listening posts or we were on ambush patrols all night.

I remember nearly falling asleep just leaning against a tree when our forward movement halted. Sometimes it could be a half hour or so before we began moving again. How easy it was just to close your eyes and fall asleep.

The Colonel had been marching us hard for nearly a week and he put an order out that we were to remain in place for a day or two. What a welcomed order that was! The enlisted men located a well. The water was amazingly clean and clear.

Moments after we set up security around our perimeter the men had their clothes off and were taking baths with this nice fresh water. By this time we all smelled like "rancid vegetable soup".

It felt so good to wash. Someone even came up with a couple bars of soap. The men splashed each other and dumped helmets full of water on each other. It was good to see them all laughing and enjoying themselves. These are the little things that help sustain morale.

A couple of men had found a tree that was in fruit. It resembled a grapefruit. It was the sweetest and most delicious fruit I had ever tasted. I had a couple of those and thanked them for sharing their find with me. This fruit tree could have been part of this villa. The owners had obviously abandoned the area because of the war or perhaps they had received word that we were in the area and were frightened off.

Although most of our searches brought us amongst the poorest of the Vietnamese, local peasants and farmers, we sometimes happen chanced upon what one might call a villa.

The house was beautiful and large by Vietnamese standards. Sometimes they were surrounded by moats and nestled in bamboo groves. I recall that one even had a beautiful wood framed bed. This was the height of luxury as most common villagers slept on mats or hammocks.

## Collateral Damage

Our artillery was often used in support of our ground operations. This was in addition to helicopter gunships that were sent in ahead of our infantry. On one such occasion I came upon an old Vietnamese woman who was unexpectedly brought to me. I could see she had been severely wounded. Her right foot was nearly severed at the ankle where a bone protruded right through her flesh at a right angle. I called for the medic and for our interpreter.

I explained to her via the interpreter that if she did not get medical treatment immediately, bacteria would set in and she could die from this injury.

She was very reluctant and untrusting. We convinced her that we would send her by helicopter to a field hospital and she would be returned to her home safely after she was properly treated.

She was very frightened of the chopper. She had never been off the ground. We found a relative who agreed to go with her. They were quickly lifted away to the hospital. I can still picture her huddled just inside the open door as the wind from the rotor whipped up the dust. She protected her face from the dust and sand with her hands. The wind furled the clothes she was wearing like a sail round a ship's mast in a winter storm.

I would never know her fate. I can only hope and pray that all went well for her. Injuries to innocent people disturbed me. The war was beginning to present me with moral questions for which I was unprepared to answer. How many more innocent women and children have we killed or maimed with all our bombs, napalm, ricochets, rockets and artillery?

## South to Ben Luc

A new mission to the south brought our company to a village called, Ben Luc. With the exception of a few "sweeps" around the area and the usual night ambush patrols, I remember Ben Luc as a rather safe haven. We even had a rock and roll group come to entertain the soldiers while we were there. Entertainment was always a welcome distraction from the daily hard grind of pushing our way through jungles and rice paddies.

The enlisted men were especially happy during these times. The lot of an enlisted man was to a large extent much more difficult than those of us who were officers. They had to perform KP (kitchen police), burn feces from the latrines and always keep their tents ready for inspection. They filled sand bags for bunkers and performed a host of other chores that were not required of officers.

Enlisted men were the ones who were the "tunnel rats".
They went down into the tunnels to "flush-out" the VC.

It was a tough, stressful and dangerous job. They also took turns as point man, leading the way up front. To be effective the point man had to be a considerable distance ahead of the rest of the platoon. As terrible as it sounds he was, to an extent, a sacrificial lamb. If there were any contact with the enemy, he might be the first to get hit. We employed this tactic to protect the main body of our force. When the point man encountered a trail or crossing he would report back to me. I would assign another man and both would walk to the right and left respectively, scouting about 100 feet on either side. They would cross and do the same on the opposite side of the trail.

Once cleared, the rest of the platoon would cross. These men were courageous. They executed orders with pride and a great deal of personal discipline. Their courage was contagious. I no longer had the same fear I had when I first arrived. Even in a firefight or skirmish I was not afraid to stand up and lead my men in an assault. Doing the right thing was all that mattered. My only concern now was the safety of my men.

*Entertainment for the troops…*

**Dinner with the Locals**

Our interpreter, Kahn, was very thin in stature. He was bright, full of "spunk" and he spoke English very well. He had managed to secure for himself a duck egg from the locals, which was considered a Vietnamese delicacy. I say "delicacy" because this egg was fertilized, with an embryo inside. That's right! He took pride in showing us, as he took a small plastic spoon and flipped the neck and head of this embryonic duck out from its shell. Ugh!

We couldn't believe he would eat it. He ate it with great relish as the rest of us turned our heads saying, "Yuk"! How separate from and ignorant of other cultures we are sometimes. We often miss the larger picture in life.

That night I was invited by some of the locals to have dinner with them. I was honored by the invitation. It was a secure area so I got permission from the CO to attend. Normally we could not be outside our perimeter of defense. I recall sitting at a long picnic table. Before the meal started, a little girl, maybe about seven or eight-years old did a Vietnamese dance on the table. She was so graceful and delightful to watch as she danced. We all gave her a round of applause when she was finished. Then the meal was served. I was given a bowl of soup containing fresh water shrimp. It was absolutely delicious. I did not wish to impose further on their generosity and ate a modest amount.

I graciously thanked them for their hospitality and went back to the confines of our base camp. The only other time I was outside the perimeter was when my interpreter friends Tuan and Kahn took me out to dinner. The restaurant was just a tiny room but the food was scrumptious.

I normally would not eat anything from the local villages for fear of becoming ill but this was a special occasion. I don't have any idea what was in those dishes but each dish was just mouth watering. It was a risk worth taking. We ate and laughed and drank the local beer. The Vietnamese are so obliging and generous. They would not allow me to pay for anything, though I offered several times. If you're their friend it's like you're part of the family.

**A Casual Conversation**

When I returned from the dinner I walked past our medic. He was sitting up on his bunk reading his bible. Walker was tall and slender as physical appearances go and was of a very quiet and gentle nature. This was a good opportunity to ask him about his religion. He was a member of the Church of the Latter Day Saints. Even though I hadn't read much of the bible we found some common ground talking about God. Although he was an enlisted man and I was an officer, our mutual faith in God brought us together. He became a special friend and I was always pleased when he was assigned to one of my patrols.

## The Mekong Delta

After Ben Luc we moved on to Rach Kien in the Mekong Delta. The landscape was flat and rich with rice paddies. They could be seen in every direction. The Mekong Delta was another infamous Viet Cong stronghold. Our company was assigned a certain sector of the perimeter of defense. From there we set out on search and destroy missions.

*Search and destroy mission...*

We had taken over some abandoned houses or "hooch's" as we called them and used them as command posts or headquarters. The hooch's were built of only one or two rooms.

The uncertainty of the war and the interference of Americans and Viet Cong in their everyday lives were incentive enough for most to give up working their beloved rice paddies.

My CP or command post was in one of these abandoned hooch's. Besides me, it included my radio operator and medic.
The arrangement, under the circumstances, was quite comfortable. Usually we were out in the open doing battle with the voracious mosquitoes and the VC. From here we sent out listening posts and ambush patrols.    There were three very disturbing events which occurred in Rach Kien. Each will forever haunt my memory.

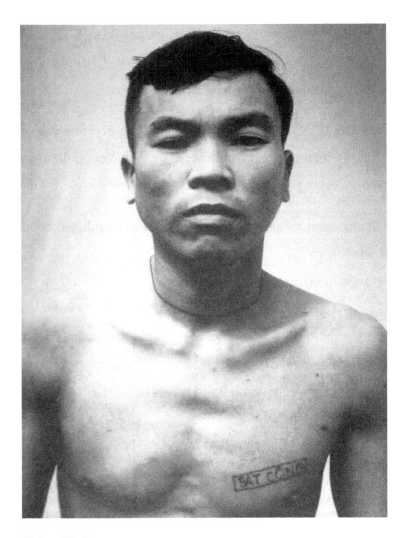

**Chieu Hoi ...**

**The First Event**

There was a guerilla group known to me at the time as the *Chieu Hoi*. They had a reputation for committing human atrocities. From what I was told and understood, the *Chieu Hoi* were former Viet Cong who had changed their allegiance back to the Saigon government and/or to the "ARVN's", an acronym for "Army of the Republic of Viet Nam". (An army which in my opinion was poorly trained, ragtime and undisciplined). To ensure that the turncoats, as one may call them, could never go back to the VC they had tattooed on their chest the words Sat Cong.

I was told that these words translated into English, meant "Kill Cong". I had seen this tattoo myself during a chance meeting with a couple of members of this guerilla group.

It was explained to me that they were paid a certain bounty (by the head) from the government for every Viet Cong they killed. If this arrangement were true, it seemed fraught with potential for the murder of innocent people.

It was a warm sunny day as usual and one of my squad leaders came excitedly to my hooch to summon me to follow him down the road to see some severed heads that were stuck to the tops of poles above some bridge.

He showed me a couple of Polaroid pictures of these heads. I was struck with horror as I looked at the long lifeless hair and sparse, straggly beards which hung from their chins. I was repulsed by what I had seen and declined his invitation to follow him to the bridge. I was told that the Chieu Hoi had done this. They were paid by the head literally. The question immediately came to my mind, "Who could prove whether or not these were just innocent farmers?" These heads could never speak the truth again nor cry out for justice much less for mercy. This war was taking some unexpected turns. My Catholic upbringing of "loving your neighbors and loving your enemies" created a deep psychological and emotional conflict within me. I felt somehow that I was responsible for this just by the fact that I was there.

I could accept fighting for my country, defending against Communism, fighting in a just war, even killing to defend oneself but I could not come to grips with the desecration of the human body, even that of my enemy.

## The Second Event

The second incident was something I witnessed first-hand. I was standing in the doorway of my headquarters when I saw a young Vietnamese male walking by our hooch. Suddenly, out of nowhere a jeep screeched to a stop just behind him. Two Vietnamese jumped out with batons like the police carry. They began beating him about the head, knocking him to the ground.

They punched him and kicked him. I wanted to intervene. Dismayed and shocked I called my company commander as this was going on right before my eyes. The CO told me that they had their own discipline and it was not our business. I was later told that he had allegedly stolen a watch or camera from one of our GI's. I thought his punishment was extreme for such a minor infraction. Then again, who knows really why he was beaten? After giving him a severe beating they put him in their jeep and drove away.

There was a small river or stream that ran adjacent to this village. Later that day around sunset, I walked over toward the stream.

I saw this same poor beaten young man crouched, in typical Vietnamese fashion, in the river with his hands tied behind his back and his head down.

I walked where he could not see me. I reached down to feel the temperature of the water. It was freezing cold. My heart sank as I stood in disbelief. I simply could not comprehend such cruelty. I thought to myself, "Perhaps I should free him." I don't recall seeing a guard.

Then my company commander's words echoed in my mind "... it's not our business." I almost could hear a voice crying out, "Guilty!" Yes, I was guilty. Everyone was guilty. This was a crime against humanity! He was a fellow human being. Our humanity was what we shared in common. I took on his shame and humiliation and the guilt of his persecutors.

Sometime later that night or in the morning he was brought to the same bridge where the heads had been hung. I was told he was shot in the head. His frail and weakened body fell into the river below. I did not witness this final act but I was told that this was his ultimate fate.

I prayed that God have mercy on his soul and for God to forgive me as well for failing to be *my brother's keeper!*

## The Third Event

The third event involved a nighttime incident with a listening post. One of the rules for engagement was that after dark anything that moved was considered to be Viet Cong.

My understanding was that the locals were informed of this rule and were to remain in their homes after dark. This rule of engagement played a major role in the incident that occurred.

*My command post ...behind which lies a dead man!*

I was enjoying the relative calm of an otherwise tranquil night. I was in my command post. A call from the LP came in on the radio. They informed me that someone was moving around just out in front of them. They wanted to know what they should do. With my rosary in hand I told them that after dark everything was fair game. Any movement after dark was considered Viet Cong. As I write this, it sounds horrible to me, "fair game." But that was the rule of engagement. I told them to kill him. They had to assume he was a Viet Cong. I went back to my rosary. A few moments later I heard a large explosion and some small arms fire coming from the direction of the LP. I called the LP and told them to return to my command post. Their position was now compromised.

The company commander was on his radio in a flash wanting to know "what the hell was going on." I told him I was on my way to find out.

The small group of three or four came directly back to the command post. The LP leader, to my shock and disbelief, held up a severed hand. They had actually cut the hand from the body with a machete. I said, "What the hell did you do that for?" His answer was "to prove we got him, sir." He went on to say that the man was trying to turn the claymore mine around towards the LP. This was a tactic the VC used with some success so that when the mine was detonated it would be facing the listening post. What he further described was not pleasant.

The man's body showed clear evidence that he was holding the claymore mine but they detonated it before he had chance to turn it toward the LP. They detonated the charge just as he had picked it up. Each member of the LP appeared shaken by the incident.

It was a close encounter and I got the sense that none of these men liked the idea of killing even though they were trained and prepared to do it. They were obviously in a heightened state of anxiety, as revealed by the ashen and pale looks on their young faces. I told the LP leader to get his men a cup of coffee, have a smoke, and to give his men a short break. I then instructed him to be prepared upon my return to go out to another location. I had other urgent business to attend to.

I had to explain this mutilation not only to my inquiring company commander as to "what the hell was going on" but also to the higher-ups, the battalion commander. To my surprise I did not catch hell. They asked me a couple questions. They wanted to know if any of our own men were wounded or killed.
They seemed to take it in stride. Maybe my face was sending messages as well.

**"Thou shall not kill…" – Holy Bible**

My mind was no longer at peace. I had given the order to kill a man. Very little emotion went into making that decision. He was dead. It was after dark. That's it. Plain and simple, dead! This is what wars are all about! We, and the enemy, get to commit murder - and it's legal. But if one looks just a tiny bit below the surface, what war is really about, is that brothers and sisters go about killing, maiming and slaughtering one another.

Can anyone deny it? Are we not all complicit? Do we not all share at least some measure of guilt in these unspeakable acts of violence? As a nation, have we not said "yes", "yes, to the political powers of government and elected officials. Whether it is a president acting on his own or with the approval of congress when all is said and done, we say a resounding and emphatic: *"Yes, we approve"!*

It was "*this particular death*" that pierced my heart and bled not blood but deep compassion. *This particular death* that opened my eyes to the brutality, cruelty and dark side of men. "We were once blind but now we can see…" – *Holy Bible* Yes, this instant transformation from life to death is now indelibly engraved on my heart, my soul and my conscience.

***This particular death*** revealed to me the fragility and preciousness of life. There is no denying TRUTH when it stands before us. There is no denying TRUTH when it is knocking at our door, staring through our eyes into our very souls. And surely there is no denying TRUTH when TRUTH cries out, "Let me in!" No, there is no denying our complicity in ***this particular death****, there is only weeping and regret!*

I was guilty even though I knew I had made the right decision. It would have been far worse if the VC had succeeded and I had three or four of my men lying dead out there. What would be the measure of *my* guilt then? I rationalized that perhaps seeing the heads stuck on those poles at the bridge played a role in their decision to mutilate this man's body. Nothing had prepared me for this. Who knew what would come next in this *insane* war?

This is a walk you walk alone. It is the spiritual wound which those whom we call veterans carry long after they have left the battlefield. It is the wound of Cain we took upon ourselves when God said, *"Cain, where is your brother, Abel?"* and like Cain, we answer, "… am I my brother's keeper?" **- Holy Bible**

## Accident at the Officers' Club

The sun was setting on the base camp. I looked forward to the happy hour in our newly constructed officers' club. The battalion commander, who was a colonel and his operations officer, a major, joined us to celebrate the opening of our new facility.

I was sitting at a table just next to them and there was a general atmosphere of relaxation. I enjoyed the end of day, not only because it brought me one day closer to the end of my tour of duty but also the general pleasure of light talk and having a few laughs to take the edge off. The gin and tonics helped a bit also.

This serene moment was broken when we heard several rounds fired in succession. To my shock, the colonel and the major both fell from their chairs seriously wounded. We all hit the floor. Somehow the VC must have infiltrated our perimeter of defense!

I jumped up and ran to my tent and got my helmet and my M16. When I came out I didn't hear any more gunfire. I ran to the officers' club and found the major and the colonel being attended to by the medics. The major had been wounded in the knee. Blood was pooled on the floor as the medics worked quickly to stop the bleeding and wrap the wounds.

They were both rushed to the field hospital. As I moved around the back of the club I found that there was a small detachment of soldiers. They were either returning from patrol or from the bunker line. It was standard procedure that once inside the base camp the order would be given to lock and clear all weapons. The round in the chamber was cleared and the weapon locked to prevent accidental discharge. Apparently, as my investigation revealed, one soldier had neglected to do so.

The small unit was being dismissed and this particular soldier's weapon discharged several rounds that went right through the screening and wood siding of the officers' club. Two officers of high rank were hit as a result. I wondered to myself how many men the VC would be willing to sacrifice to get two such high ranking officers, one a battalion commander and the other his S3 operations officer. We saved them the bother. Leave us to ourselves, I thought, and we would win the war for them. I was becoming bitter. Accidents like this enraged me. I tried to dismiss it by thinking, "they were rookies. Accidents are bound to happen. "

A couple of days later I went to the hospital to visit the Colonel and the Major. The Colonel, although tough, was a very forgiving man. He saw it as purely an accident. I was taken aback by his dismissive attitude of the incident. I thought there should be some punitive action taken against this soldier for his carelessness. "How could he have been so stupid", I thought to myself. He should be punished in some way. The colonel's level of wisdom eluded me.

My youth and strict upbringing had taught me to see things as black and white, good or bad, right or wrong. There were no gray areas. Life was simple when you could get along if everyone just followed the rules. My views on events were infantile. I had a lot to learn about life.

## R & R (Rest and Recreation) in Honolulu Hawaii

Finally my turn arrived for R&R. Many of the soldiers went to Vung Tau, Taiwan or Taipei for their R&R. Some of us chose instead to travel to the Hawaiian Islands. I chose Oahu. I wanted to share Hawaii with my wife, Jan. I was told that the hotels there were exquisite.

I wrote to Jan and she made plans to meet me there on Oahu. Jan made our hotel reservations and booked her flight from Boston. All the exclusive named hotels like the Ilikai were booked solid. She had to settle for something mid-range. It didn't matter. All that mattered was that we would be together for five days.

We hadn't seen each other in six months. To me it seemed like six years. After our plane touched down we disembarked. We were all gathered into a large auditorium. I could see Jan amongst the eager crowd but we were not allowed to break ranks until we were properly dismissed. We were lectured on the "dos'" and "don'ts" of our visit to the Island. We were advised of sexually transmitted diseases. We were advised about our return time etc. Finally we were formally dismissed.

How precious it was to hold the one I loved in my arms once again. We talked about our daughter Michelle. We had five days to spend together. I was so proud that Jan had the courage to fly all the way from Boston by herself to meet me in such a far off place for just five days. We shopped a little. We went to the beach and had wonderful quiet and romantic dinners together.

We participated in a Luau where we all sat on the floor and ate scrumptious servings of local Hawaiian food. Everyone was dressed in bright colored clothes. We especially liked Waikiki beach with the view of Diamondhead stretching out to the sea like a dark and forbidding giant. I felt so free again. This sense of freedom was short lived. Five days is a brief time.

Soon it was time to say "goodbye" again. I was concerned for her flight back alone. I prayed to God to keep her safe. After we parted I felt such loneliness. I still had several months to serve in Vietnam. I wasn't out of the woods yet.

**Headquarters Executive Officer**

A few months after my promotion, I was re-assigned as Headquarters Company Executive Officer. I was replaced by a fresh, new lieutenant. I was now in the relative safety of the base camp. It turned out to be a most boring assignment. Crazy as it may seem I wanted to be out there where the action was. I think there was a certain high I got from living on the edge.

I missed that rush. Perhaps I had gotten addicted to the constant adrenalin. The base camp by comparison was hot, dry, dusty and desolate. I also felt uneasy about entrusting my platoon to someone else. I missed being their platoon leader.

I sat in an office learning how to reconcile the company's cash account. I had a degree in business but had difficulty figuring out exactly what I was supposed to do. Even the procedures I read didn't make sense to me. I found myself waiting for five p.m. every afternoon when the beer delivery came. Cans of beer embedded in ice and rice husks. The husks were added to keep it cool. One thing this assignment did give me was the opportunity to research how to qualify for an "early out". If you were accepted into a graduate program you could receive a so-called "early out". This would shorten my tour of duty. I sent a letter to Boston College to apply for their Graduate School of Management Program.

## La Verne Walker

It was early evening and I was sitting outside my tent. The sun was setting, a welcome relief from the scorching hot day. I was reading and re-reading the letters I received from Jan.

She was so faithful, sending me a letter every single day. I devoured each word, somehow trying to re-live the closeness we had shared on R&R in Hawaii. The longing and waiting was insufferable. What about our baby, Michelle? I wanted to hold her in my arms and be a daddy once again. She was only four months old when I left. Would she even let me hold her? How would she respond to this stranger who would abruptly re-enter her life?

While musing on all of these thoughts, one of the men silently dropped off a duffle bag right in front of where I was sitting. I opened it with trepidation and there at the very top of all the personal belongings was a small New Testament Bible.

I recognized it instantly as Walker's, the medic. I couldn't believe it. I felt numb. He only had this last operation and then he was to be taken off the line. Later, upon inquiry, I found out that he had tripped a booby trap and was fatally wounded.

How strange a feeling it is when you know that one of your men is dead and his spouse doesn't know yet. I knew that within a short time she would know. I could feel the depth of her loss; that hollow, empty feeling when a soul mate has died never to be seen or spoken to again. What pain I felt for her. What heartache she would endure at having lost such a wonderful husband. Grief that only others like her could possibly understand.

I felt I had failed him. I had mentioned several times to the company commander that he had been on the line for a long time. I was assured this would be his last operation. I was so angry! If they had only taken him off the line when I told them he would still be alive! He came on many of my ambush patrols, night after night. He never complained. Walker was a gentle, loving soul. He impressed me most with his personal devotion to God, his faith and his love for his wife.

**Incoming Medical Evacuation**

A chopper came in unexpectedly one evening just after dark. They placed the wounded soldier by himself in a tent. I went immediately into the tent to see who had been brought in and if there was anything I could do for him. I knew the soldier. He was a member of my old platoon. His name was Sanchez. The flesh on his thighs, chest and arms appeared as though they had exploded from the inside out. He had stepped on a booby trap. His face looked grey. He appeared to be going into shock. When I approached him he immediately recognized me and said, "I'm all 'F***'d up', sir". I wanted to be encouraging. I told him he'd be okay but I was really afraid he might die.

Why did the pilot drop him off here? We had no facilities to treat this type of injury in the company area. Maybe he had to return to get more wounded. Who knows? I waited with Sanchez until we could transport him to the field hospital. I could only comfort him by simply being there. I kept telling him he'd be okay. I felt so helpless. I don't know if he ever made it. Anger, pain and frustration magnified my sense of powerlessness.

We were told that we were here to fight the spread of Communism. Were we really winning this war? I sure didn't think so.

I remembered that old cliché, *"War is hell!"* I found out that it really is! It is hell, not only because precious flesh and blood are destroyed, but what war does to your mind. The mind cannot fathom such depths of doubt, questioning, contradictions, events, love and hate, brotherhood, despair, courage, weakness, life, human suffering and death.

## Thoughts Running Through My Head

I served a couple more months as Company Executive Officer. Time crept by slowly. The days and weeks that followed gave me much pause for thought and time for reflection. I was now a "short timer".

Like a movie running through my mind were the wet nights on patrol. The many nights we spent curled up in a makeshift foxhole trying to keep warm. Our fatigues soaked through to the skin. Mosquitoes by the hoards buzzed incessantly, hour after interminable hour, trying desperately to get at our fresh flesh for a meal.

I could still feel the rush of adrenalin as I recalled the choppers dropping us into hot landing zones.

I could still picture the awesome helicopter gunships as they swiftly moved in ahead of us firing rockets and the door gunners blasting away at the tree lines to give us cover.

I could still hear the sound of a weapon called "The Cyclops" in Cu Chi which fired round after round in the night to harass and interdict the enemy.

I pictured the tunnels and the caches of weapons we found.

I recalled peaceful moments too when you could take a shower (cold water of course) and feel fresh and human again.

There were the good times at the officer's club, a place where you could have a drink with a friend.

I thought of my Vietnamese friend and interpreter Tuan. I knew I would never see him again. We became good friends. He was younger than I, very much like a younger brother. He planned to come to the States to attend a university when his tour of duty was over. I hope he fulfilled his dream.

My thoughts turned to the convoys passing through Saigon, Ben Luc and Rach Kien, a vista of beautiful and otherwise peaceful countryside.

There were the old men and boys who tilled the fields behind the water buffalo and plough. The women who planted rice in the wet fields with their pant legs rolled up to their knees. Women squatted down on the side of the road to suckle their babies.

I recall one little boy, about nine or ten years old, who held the tether of a water buffalo that decided to run off. The child held on for dear life trying to restrain him. He finally let go of the tether. He certainly was no match for his buffalo. He fell down with his body stretched out in the wet rice paddy. He quickly got to his feet to continue the chase. I must confess it was a comical sight and did give us a laugh.

There were the beautiful sunrises and sunsets that danced delicately and gracefully through the bamboo leaves. I marveled at it all.

There was the old woman whose ankle had been shattered by our artillery.

Then there were the children always smiling and laughing as we passed by.

*"Unless you become like little children …" – Holy  Bible*

***There was the smiling Vietnamese girl tenderly carrying her
little brother ...***

Intermingled with these recollections was the growing awareness
of newspaper articles about the anti-war movement which was
increasing day by day at home. That never weakened our resolve.
We were fighting for our country, for our lives and for one another.

At this moment in history, my moment in history, we were at war.
We were proud. We were committed. The stakes were high.
Many had given their lives. Life and death were locked tightly in
an ever-unpredictable embrace.

Also running through my mind was guilt, "Why him and not me?" What right did I have to live? Why was his body placed in a body bag instead of mine? Why should his family grieve when mine will rejoice? I wasn't wounded or killed. I was still alive. Perhaps I didn't give my all. Unanswered questions – *"but for the grace of God, there go I!"*

## Going Home

When I returned from R&R in Hawaii I found on my bunk fifty copies of discharge orders. My discharge from active duty was May 26, 1967. I had been accepted into Boston College's Graduate Program. I was going home! My hope now was simply to stay alive until that day came. I had heard tales of soldiers who with only days to go, sometimes even hours, were killed by mortars lobbed into the air base.

After several more weeks my turn finally arrived. I wore my best khakis. My shirt was now decorated with ribbons and medals including my bronze star. I proudly wore a light blue infantry cord around my shoulder. It was another proud moment for me. I said goodbye to the few that I knew who were still in the base camp.

As I walked by the tents of Alpha Company for the last time, I passed by some new recruits who had just arrived in country.

They were just sitting on the ground awaiting their assignments. They looked so young to me, perhaps only eighteen or nineteen years of age. I felt I had grown so old. I was now a veteran. I studied their young faces as I walked by, returning their salute.

I suffered for them because I knew some would never go home. Others would be wounded. And then there would be those who by luck, by fate or by God's kindness and mercy would find their way home again.

The remnants of my old platoon were out in the field with a new lieutenant, new sergeants and new replacements. Sgt. Zuck, Sgt. Belcher, Sgt. Lewis, Sgt. Sheffield and Sgt.Terrian, along with many of the others had rotated home before me. I would never see them again. Everything was changed now. I had changed. I wasn't the person I used to be. I knew I was different - very different.

My term of active duty had come to a close. The camaraderie was over. The brotherhood dissolved. I was on my own. I was to become a civilian again. I felt a deep sense of loss, loneliness, anxiety and disconnectedness. I felt a profound emptiness.

## Flight to Bien Hoa

A helicopter was reserved to fly me to Bien Hoa Airport. I was to take a commercial flight out of Vietnam within the next few days. I boarded the chopper and off I went for the last time. The breeze coming in the open door was refreshing. I was on my way.

We flew for some time and then came upon a large open area. I could see off in the distance, on a slight ridge, a set of Quonset huts. The pilot set the chopper down and I eagerly jumped out with my bag in hand.

I ran up the hill toward the buildings. I opened the door and walked inside. There was a sergeant who stood behind a long counter. I asked him if this was Bien Hoa. To my shock and dismay he told me that I was not at Bien Hoa! He told me I could take a bus which ran every hour or so. My heart sank. Did the pilot not know where I was going? Did I get off too soon? Was there some misunderstanding?

I turned my head back to the field and I saw another chopper coming in. I did not want to take a bus. I ran down the hill as fast as I could and waived frantically at the pilot of this incoming chopper.

I caught his attention and he landed, the rotors still turning as I yelled out to him, "I need to get to Bien Hoa!"

He said, "Hop in, I'll take you there." A short time later I was at Bien Hoa Airbase. I gratefully bid my generous pilot goodbye and walked towards the central area of the airstrip.

I found several buildings surrounded by sandbags. I walked into what appeared to be an office building and showed them my set of orders. In return they simply directed me to a holding area of small cabins. Inside were wooden beds. I was to remain here until my flight home arrived. I hoped it wouldn't be too long because I didn't want to be one of those "on the way home" casualties I had heard so much about.

There was nothing to do but wait. After scouting around a little I found a club with a bar. I relished the idea of being nearly free of it all and heralded this moment as a cause for a personal celebration. So I gave a toast to myself for a job well done. Better yet, for keeping myself alive and being able to raise a glass at all.

A Vietnamese rock and roll group was entertaining at the bar. It consisted of two or three men and a female singer. The men played guitar and drums and the young lady in her very mini-skirt sang Roy Orbison's song, "*Pretty Woman*". However my thoughts were on home and my re-union with Jan. It was just a long flight away before I would see her and hold her for real in my arms. I thought of Michelle and how much she had grown since I last saw her. How much she and I had missed during my long absence and her first year of life.

A couple of nights went by. The wooden beds proved to be even more uncomfortable than what I had become used to lying in foxholes or bunker line duty. Early one morning we saw a commercial aircraft approaching the airport. As the landing gear came down we could make out the colors of red and white. In its final descent we identified the aircraft as TWA. After it landed it taxied to a stop on the tarmac. Word went out that this was the aircraft that would take us home. Everyone began to shout and cheer.

**The Flight Home**

The aircraft was refueled and otherwise prepared. We boarded, as directed, in a very orderly fashion. We were finally going home! The engines started and we taxied to the departure line. Soon the pilots were revving the engines. Louder and louder they roared as we sped down the runway. As soon as the wheels left the ground cheers rang out again. The plane echoed with roars of laughter.

Every soldier's face was a picture of joy. The stewardesses were quick to come around with steaming hot facecloths. We all rested our heads back and breathed great sighs of relief. We were out of Vietnam and heading home.

After the initial hoorahs, things settled down. Quiet conversations could be heard between individuals and small groups.
The constant hum of the aircraft lulled some of us to sleep or to doze. I don't recall our route home. Perhaps it was the reverse of how I had arrived. I felt a growing anxiety that the plane would crash and I would never make it home. A different kind of fear was building within me. It just seemed to be overwhelming me. My anxiety was so severe.

After our touchdown in the States, we all got off and we boarded different planes to take us to our respective home states. Civilians now filled the aircraft. My military family, my brothers; my comrades in arms were all gone now. I was alone in the midst of strangers. I was crying out from within, "Do you know where I just came from? Only hours ago I was in Vietnam!" I tried to strike up some conversation. I even told a couple of people that I was just coming home from Vietnam. Their faces barely broke a smile as they read books or newspapers or chatted amongst themselves. What did I expect? I wanted them to know.

I wanted them to care. So I came home the way I went - alone, frightened and feeling very disconnected.

My sense of pride for having served my country in combat was quickly disintegrating. All the soldiers who lost their lives or their limbs were fading away as though it was my own personal nightmare. I was trapped between two realities - the reality of war and the reality of indifference from those for whom we fought it. I consoled myself with thoughts of seeing my family. I hoped at least they would be proud of me.

After hours of flying, Boston's Logan Airport was finally on the horizon. Crazy thoughts ran through my head: "Would the plane crash as we land?" Will it just explode in mid-air?" "Will I really make it home?" I couldn't contain the frantic emotions whirling around inside me.

I was almost in a state of panic. Despite my fears to the contrary, the plane landed safely. When I disembarked my eyes quickly scanned across the many faces that were waiting.

There she was. She looked lovelier than I could have dreamed. Jan came rushing towards me. We kissed and embraced. I hadn't felt such softness, such tenderness in such a long time.

I wanted to hold Michelle but I didn't want to frighten her. Jan said that she was somewhat shy about going to strangers. I extended my arms out to her. After a moment's hesitation she reached out her arms. I held her and kissed her. How beautiful and soft she was. She let me carry her into the terminal before she became restless for her mother. Some of Jan's relatives were there to greet me. It was a happy reunion. I was home at last.

**Welcome Home**

My mother and father held a small "Welcome Home" party for me at their home in Malden, Massachusetts. Later Jan and I slipped away together to our new apartment. Michelle stayed with Jan's mom for a couple of days. It was time for us to begin our lives again.

A few days later, my father-in-law took me to his favorite pub on Dorchester Avenue, a place called, Vaughn's. My father-in-law, Carl, was relatively shy in social circles so I was surprised when he introduced me as his son-in-law who just came back from Vietnam. I could feel my pride rising up within but it was quickly crushed. "Oh," said one man, "that's not a war!"

"The real war was WWII," said another. I felt ashamed. I was not welcomed here. Had we not given enough? Was the blood that we shed in Vietnam less precious than the blood that was shed in World War II? I visualized a large door. I reached out and grabbed it by its handle and slammed it shut. I promised myself I would never open it again ...until today.

## Civilian Life

I felt a sense of boredom with civilian life. It felt as though everyone else was alive but I was dead. I missed the excitement of combat. Nothing could compare with the rush you get from putting your life on the line. Working in an office just didn't compare to that level of intensity and that heightened state when all your senses are alert and alive.

I went through some hard times. On several occasions, at the sound of a firecracker I would hit the floor, literally. I could not control this reflex action. Even today I have flashbacks on Fourth of July. I suffered some Post Traumatic Stress Disorder.

I experienced panic attacks. I was diagnosed by a psychiatrist as having anxiety neurosis when I was in my thirties. I also suffered flare-ups in temper. Alcohol and Valium became my medications.

I had difficulty adapting to my new world. I developed a bad attitude and a bit of a chip on my shoulder. Sadly our marriage ended after twenty-four years. I was hurting the ones I loved the most.

## Afterthoughts

History has taught me that the Vietnam War was not *our* war. It was a political war grown from an exaggerated fear of the spread of Communism. We were unfortunate enough to be caught up in it. We were just *their* grunts, political pawns. We were *their* boots on the ground. It was up to us to win *their* war. *Their* military mission was always the same. Search and destroy; find, engage and kill the enemy! Politicians determined our fate in Vietnam.

*Our* personal mission was a different one. Kill or be killed, look after one another and make your way home. *Our* war was staying alive moment to moment. It was the rice paddies, the jungles and the rubber tree plantations. It was ambush patrols, booby traps, tunnels, air assaults and search and destroy missions. It was a war of going without sleep and of scorching heat, sweat, rain, mud and mosquitoes. It was living with the constant thought of knowing your next step could be your last. It was the experience of grief and sorrow for a fallen comrade. Finally it was a war of endless searches for a cunning, underestimated, unseen, courageous and elusive enemy.

Our frequent lack of success became a breeding ground for my deep personal anger, rage, frustration and heightened anxiety. I could see how much I had changed. I had lost my fear of killing. Perhaps it is true that a man *can* become the very thing he hates.

## An Invitation

I was invited by my boss at work to attend a business conference in Alexandria, Virginia. I knew that on my own I would never get the opportunity to see in person the Vietnam Memorial Wall. I also knew deep down inside that I still had not put closure on La Verne's death. I hadn't mourned for him and there was no way for me to pay my respects to his wife for his great sacrifice. I invited my wife Helene to come along on this trip because I did not know how I might react emotionally and quite honestly I needed her support.

During one of the extended breaks in the conference Helene and I went to the Wall. I was afraid I might not find his name or that for some reason it just wouldn't be there. My fears were quickly allayed when we found his name after only a brief search. I wept silently as I touched his name with my hand. I wore my military cap with insignia along with my awards for my service. I stood back at attention and saluted my farewell salute not only to La Verne but also to everyone who gave their lives. I felt less somehow than those who had paid the ultimate price. To me they were the real heroes of this most regrettable war. La Verne was an avid reader of his bible and clearly a man of peace. He never took a weapon on operations or patrols. In his memory I would like to dedicate this hopeful verse from scripture:

***In Memoriam***

***Isaiah Chapter 2, verse 4.***

***"… and they shall beat their swords into plowshares, and their spears into pruning forks: nation shall not lift up sword against nation, neither shall they learn war anymore."***

**La Verne Walker (medic)**          *Right panel 15th down from top*

25th Infantry Division
Cu Chi, Vietnam

**August 1966 - May 1967**

1ˢᵗ *Lieutenant Fredric A. Voto*
*Cu Chi, Vietnam*

**2ⁿᵈ of the 14ᵗʰ**        **Tropic** Lightning

**War as Suffering**

I am now sixty-nine years old. Our country has just emerged from two wars, Iraq and Afghanistan. We have lost over four thousand men and women, thousands wounded, homeless, blind, mentally ill, brain damaged and dismembered. There are tens of thousands of innocent civilians who have been killed, maimed or displaced. Whole families have been destroyed. Health care for returning veterans has been a dismal national disgrace. The suicide rate among our troops is soaring. Drones splatter the flesh and blood of innocent civilians across the sands of the Middle East. We lost over 50,000 of America's finest young men and women in Vietnam.

It seems to me that those who rattle sabers and rush to war; who see war as a solution instead of the intrinsic evil and sickness that it is; with few exceptions, never send their own children to fight them.

They send someone else's children to fight instead. And who are they? They are to a large extent the poor, the disenfranchised and underprivileged.

Few members of our Congress have been in combat nor have they experienced the many discomforts and human sufferings that go hand in hand with war.

I salute each and every soldier, sailor, marine and airman who has given his all and for the thousands more who will meet with violent death. I share the pain and suffering of the families whose lives will never be the same; whose wounds will never heal.

**A Different Perspective: America's Need to Encounter Its Shadow**

I would like to close with these quotations from Richard Rohr, O.F.M., A Franciscan Priest and from His Holiness, the Dalai Lama:

*Richard Rohr* - "All over the world you can sense a growing awareness of the dignity of the individual. There is a growing distrust of power, dictatorships and mechanisms of oppression. But our country is built on a mythology of power, and it will be very hard to deprive the system of its power. America has to acknowledge its shadow. I believe the Vietnam War was the encounter with our shadow, but we forgot about it too quickly." [1]

*Richard Rohr"* "… I've told gatherings in Germany that because many Germans have never repented the Second World War, they're going to repeat it. It is as certain as the dawn that America will continue to be a militaristic, violent country because we have

---

[1] . *Simplicity - The Freedom of Letting Go by Richard Rohr, O.F.M. p. 135.*

*English translation copyright 1991.*

*By The Crossroad Publishing Company.*

never repented any of our wars. Grief and repentance are the only appropriate Christian response to *any* war, never a victory parade. At very best, wars are a necessary evil, which we can never celebrate or romanticize." [2]

## How to See Yourself As You Really Are

*The Dalai Lama* - "The world is becoming smaller now, to the degree that all parts of the world are obviously part of yourself. Thus destruction of your enemy is destruction of yourself.
The very concept of war is outdated. If the twentieth century was the century of bloodshed, the twenty-first has to be the century of dialogue".[3]

---

[2] *Jesus' Plan for a New World by Richard Rohr with John Feister p. 108 .*

*Copyright 1966 Richard Rohr and John Feister*

*Published by St Anthony Messenger Press*

[3] *How to See Yourself As You Really Are p. 9.*

*Copyright 2006 by His Holiness the Dalai Lama*

*Published by Atria Books, New York*

## About the Author - Fredric A. Voto

I am now retired with my wife and soul mate, Helene. We plan to live our final days here in the pleasant countryside of Connecticut. I work part-time in a local community hospital.

The idea for writing *"Vietnam ... One Soldier's Experience"* was born out of my forty-seven year need to tell my story. Although it is neither a war story filled with great heroic battles nor an historical, chronological narrative; it depicts a very real, personal experience of the fighting and types of operations that we conducted in Vietnam during 1966-1967 and the profound effects it had on my life and the lives of tens of thousands of ordinary young men and women who said "yes" to serving their country.

## Vietnam - The Silent War

Vietnam was "the silent war". Our enemy did not possess powerful weapons such as Germany had in WWII. The myth of war, as we Americans understand it, did not apply to Vietnam. Jungle or guerilla warfare is not conventional. Vietnam was "the silent war" because our enemy used stealth, concealment, creative imagination and cunning. They were elusive far beyond what our generals could have imagined. The Viet Cong were invisible on the battlefield; tenacious and courageous in their tunnels. They were heroic in their fervor to defeat their enemy; to seize their country's sovereignty and shape its own destiny. What is it that we can't seem to learn from Vietnam? An administration's lies and deceptions seduced us as we blundered our way into Iraq. Subsequently we miscalculated the determination and resistance from the Taliban and Al Qaida forces in Afghanistan. Fools rush in where wise men never tread!

Are we blind to the ruthless and brutal murder and killing of innocent men, women and children across the globe? Can we not see the horrific slaughter of our own children, our own flesh and blood that we are so willing to sacrifice them to a misguided and misinformed government. Have we as a nation grown immune to the savagery and merciless blood-letting that is war? Has America lost forever the virtues of love, peace and compassion which are the foundation for peaceful dialogue and diplomacy and which define a truly great and ***enlightened*** nation?

*Prayer for Peace*

*May Almighty God take away our blindness*

*and pour His heavenly light into our darkness*

*that all mankind SHALL NOT BE blind, but that they*

*may SEE ...*

# ᾺΩ

Footnotes:

1. *Simplicity - The Freedom of Letting Go by Richard Rohr,*

   *O.F.M. p. 135. English translation copyright 1991. By The Crossroad Publishing      Company.*

2. *Jesus' Plan for a New World by Richard Rohr with John Feister p. 108 .*

*Copyright   1966 Richard Rohr and John Feister*

*Published by St Anthony Messenger Press*

3. *How to See Yourself As You Really Are p. 9.*

*Copyright  2006 by His Holiness the Dalai Lama*

*Published by Atria Books, New York*

 4.  *Bible Lk. 18:8*

5.  *Ibid.  Lv. 19:18*

6.  *Ibid.  Mt. 5:44*

7.  *Ibid Jn. 15:13*

Made in the USA
Middletown, DE
02 September 2021